▲ 필자 近影

조선문학 수필선 4

유·설·자·수·필·집

도레미 파솔라 시도의 합창

The Making of a 'Do Re Mi Fa So La Ti Do' Choir

by Sul Ja, Yoo

조선문학사

내 심상의 카타르시스(Katharisis), 글쓰기

나는 학창시절부터 글쓰기를 좋아 했다. 또한 이 세상에 존재하는 모든 아름다운 것들을 사랑 한다. 가시밭길 이민생활에서도 틈틈이 글을 쓸 수 있었다는 것은 하나님이 주신 크나큰 은사임에 틀림없다. 이 험한 세상에서 자칫 흐트러지려는 내 심상을 카타르시스(Katharisis) 할 수 있는 글쓰기는 항상 나를 행복의 호수로 유인 한다.

이제 지나온 내 반생을 뒤 돌아보며 은사로 주신 여덟 명의 손주들의 이야기와 여행기록을 엮어 모았다. 온 세계를 두루 두루 돌아보며 인생에서 필요한 많은 것을 터득 했다.

나에게 문학의 길로 이끌어 주신 조선문학의 박진환 박사님과 해외문학의 조윤호 회장님께 무한한 감사를 드린다. 수년간 지면을 허락해

주신 워싱턴한국일보, 늘 사랑과 격려를 주신 워싱턴한국일보 정영희 기자님, 권기팔 기자님께 무한한 감사를 드린다.

부족한 글들을 한 권의 책으로 나오기 까지 출간을 도와준 조선문학사에도 감사를 드린다. 내게 사랑을 느끼게 해준 사랑하는 문우들과 워싱턴 여류수필가협회 회원들, 미주문예동우회 회원들에게도 고마움을 전한다.

끝으로 묵묵히 외조를 아끼지 않았던 남편과 늘 희망과 용기를 주는 두 딸가족에게 감사와 사랑을 전한다.

이 모든 길을 마련해주신 무한한 하나님의 사랑에 큰 영광을 올려드린다.

미국 Washington DC 에서

유 설 자

축복된 문운이 있기를

내가 아는 유설자씨와는 아주 인연이 깊다.

같은 교회에 나가면서 알게 되었고 또한 같이 글쓰기를 좋아하는 이라서 쉽게 친해졌다.

성격이 활달하고 재주가 많으며 뭐든지 열성을 다해 노력하는 성품이 나를 사로 잡았다.

동생처럼 뭐든지 거리낌 없는 친숙함이며 글쓰기에도 열정을 다 해서 배우며 쓰고 또 써서 좋은 글을 쓰게 되는 것 같다.

왕성한 젊음을 과시 하듯 세계 여행을 즐기며 아주 많은 여행기록을 남겼다.

특히 여덟이나 되는 햇병아리 같은 손자 손녀들을 키우고 돌보면서 아주 행복하고 다복한 부부애를 자랑한다.

우리들의 귀감이 되고도 남음이 있다.

같은 길을 가는 문인으로서 자랑스러우며 또한 앞으로 축복된 문운이 있기를 간절히 바라 마지 않는다.

시인 · 수필가 / 미주 문예동우회 회장

손 지 언

CONTENTS

제2부

제3부

제4부

제5부

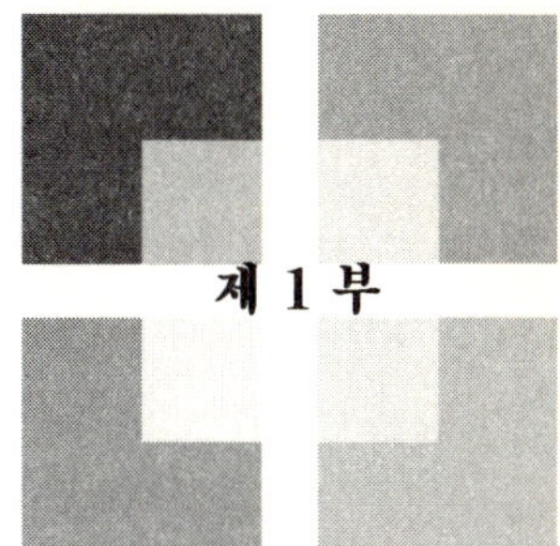

제 1 부

어머니를 그리는 마음

Longing for Mother

밖에는 봄비가 부슬부슬 제법 소리를 내며 내리는 늦은 밤이다. 남편은 피곤하다며 일찍 잠자리에 들고 우리 귀염둥이 강아지 뽀삐도 내곁에 길게 누워 단잠에 빠져 있다.

갑자기 쓸쓸해지는 내 마음 한가운데 이 세상에 안계신 친정어머니를 향한 그리움이 가득 채워지면서 내 눈에 이슬이 맺힌다.

유난히도 피부가 뽀얗고 고우셔서 나이보다 젊어 보이셨고 다정다감 하시며 섬기는 교회에서 여전도회장으로 궂은 일은 남이 할세라 앞장서서 일하셨던 어머니, 김효성 집사님!

1974년 9월25일, 그러니까 33년전 어머니는 58세의 비교적 이른 나이에 아버지와 우리 육남매를 남겨둔채 하늘나라로 떠나셨다. 그때 막내 남동생이 15살 중학생이었다. 어머니는 1년의 투병생활끝에 돌아가실 때 눈도 제대로 못감고 가셨단다. 어린 자식을 두고 가자니 얼마나 안타깝고 억울하고 슬펐겠는가…

당시 미국에서 생활하던 나는 어머니가 위독하시다는 전화를 받고 황급히 짐을 챙겨서 생후 6개월된 딸 아이를 데리고 고국으로 가는 비행기를 탔다.

4살난 큰아이는 아빠 곁에 남겨둔채 금방 돌아올 것이라 기대하고 말이다. 그때만 해도 직행하는 비행기가 없어 L.A를 거쳐 장장 20여 시간은 더 걸렸던 것 같다. 그런데도 아기는 슬픈 내 마음을 읽기나 한 듯 내 품에서 잠자며 보채지도 않았다.

비행기안에서 나는 '우리 어머니 꼭 살려주세요.' 라고 하나님께 간절히 애원하며 긴 기도를 드리고 또 드렸다.

병상에 계신 어머니는 지칠대로 지치고 쇠약한 몸으로 큰 딸인 나를 반겨주셨다. 처음 보는 손녀딸을 힘겹게 겨우 안아보시기도 하시며 베이비 음식을 잘 받아먹는 손녀딸을 물끄러미 쳐다보시기도 했다. 어머니의 상태는 좋아지는 것 같다가도 다시 나빠져 온 집안이 초상집이었다. 금방 돌아가실 듯 엄청난 고통에서 헤매시는 어머니의 그 아픔은 차마 눈으로 볼 수 없었다. 나는 어머니곁을 지키며 '하나님 우리 어머니를 빨리 데려가세요. 저 고통에서 어서 해방시켜 주세요' 라고 수없이 눈물을 흘리며 기도 드렸다.

그런데 4살난 딸 아이를 직장 다니는 남편에게 맡기고 왔으니 마냥 있을 수가 없었다. 나는 어머니에게 큰 아이를 데리고 다시 오겠다고 조심스럽게 말했다. 그런데 어머니는 미소를 띄시며 "그래 잘가라, 조심해서" 라고만 했지 꼭 오라고는 안하셨다. 전에는 "죽든지 살든지 꼭 보고 가라"며 떼(?)를 쓰던 어머니가 아니었던가. 어머니는 바로 큰 딸과의 마지막 작별의 시간이 됐음을 미리 아신 것 같았다.

미국에 돌아와서 12일이 지난후 막 잠자리에 들때였다. 따르릉 전화소리에 놀라 수화기를 들었다. 오빠의 슬픈 목소리가 전화기 너머로 흘러나왔다.

"어머니께서 오늘 정오에 별세하셨다 . 그 엄청난 아픔에서 해방되어 하나님곁에 가셨으니 너무 슬퍼하지 말아라." 전화를 끊고 난 나는 순식간에 마음이 편안해짐을 느꼈다. 정말이지 어머니가 그 엄청난 고통에서 해방되었다니 얼마나 감사한 일인가. 하나님께 진심으로 감사를 드리며 오랜만에 편한 마음으로 잠을 잘 수 있었다.

그러나 그 다음날부터 나는 걷잡을 수 없는 허탈감에 빠지고 있었다. 어머니가 이 세상 어디에도 안계신다고 생각하니 눈물이 비오듯 쏟아졌다. 엉엉 소리내며 울고 또 울었다. 12일만 더 어머니 곁에 있었더라면 어머니의 마지막 모습도 지켜볼 수 있었을거고 장례에도 참여할 수 있었을텐데 뒤늦은 후회가 밀물처럼 밀려왔다.

수많은 세월속에서도 어머니를 생각하면 나의 눈은 어느 틈에 눈물로 가득 채워진다.

이제 우리 6남매는 미국에 넷, 한국에 둘 비록 이산가족이지만 모두 잘 살고 있는데 정작 효도받으셔야할 어머니는 우리 곁에 더 이상 안계신다. 이제는 아버지도 이 세상에 안계신다. 서둘러 달려갔을 때 아버지는 혼수상태에 계셨다. 잠시 정상으로 돌아오셔서 주위에 앉은 아들, 며느리, 딸, 사위들을 둘러보시고 눈을 감으셨다. 아버지는 14년만에 어머니 곁에 나란히 묻히셨는데 어머니와 합장(合葬)하던 날, 합장을 하기 위해 파 놓은 무덤안에서 난 어머니의 관을 볼 수 있었다.

생전의 어머니를 만난 듯 어머니관을 향하여 '임종을 지켜드리지 못한 큰 딸이 이제야 어머니를 찾아왔어요' 라고 사죄를 드렸다. 어머니! 33년

전 불편한 몸으로 안아주셨던 생후 6개월이었던 어머니의 손녀딸이 지금은 어엿한 세 아이의 엄마가 됐어요. '어머니, 오늘 이밤이 지나고 나면 어머니의 고통스러웠던 슬픈 추억일랑 모두 내 머리에서 지워버릴거에요. 건강하셨을 때 어머니의 환한 모습과 즐거웠던 좋은 추억만을 간직하며 살 것입니다. 사랑하는 어머니! 꿈속에서라도 한번 뵐 수는 없을까요--- 어머니! 너무나 그립습니다.'

It was late at night. I could hear the gentle sound of spring rain falling outside. My husband said he was tired and retired to bed early. Even our darling little puppy, Bopey, lay fast asleep at my side.

Overcome with a feeling of melancholy, suddenly I feel tears in my eyes as my heart fills with longing thoughts of my deceased mother. Such exceptionally fair, white skin that belied her years. So sentimental. Always taking the initiative to do the dirty work at the church she served as president of the women's missionary association. Deacon Kim Hyoseong -- Mother!

It was 33 years ago on September 25, 1974, when at the relatively young age of 58 she left her husband and six children to be with God in heaven. The youngest child was my 15-year-old brother, a middle-school student. When Mother passed away after a one-year battle with illness, they say she couldn't even close her eyes completely. How heartbroken, hurt, and sad she must have been knowing she had to leave behind her young children.

I was living in America when I received the phone call informing me that Mother's condition was grave. I hastily packed my bags and boarded a plane for Korea with my 6-month-old daughter in my arms. I left my older daughter with her father, as I knew I couldn't be gone too long. There were no direct flights to Korea back then, so we had to make a stop in L.A., which made the trip last more than 20 hours. My daughter seemed to sense the sadness in my heart and just slept quietly in my bosom. On the plane, I passionately petitioned God with a barrage of long prayers. I just prayed, "Please, Lord, let Mother live."

Mother was delighted to see me, her oldest daughter, but she looked totally exhausted and very frail there in her bed. She had barely enough strength to hold the granddaughter she was viewing for the first time, and then stared vacantly at my daughter devouring her baby food.

The entire family seemed like a family mourning as Mother's condition wavered between seeming to improve and getting worse. I couldn't bear watching her suffer through the excruciating pain as she hovered between life and death. I stood vigil beside her, weeping and praying, "God, please just take her quickly. Free her from this pain, oh Lord."

Having left my four-year-old daughter with my husband, who had to keep working, I couldn't stay with Mother indefinitely. With reservation I told her that I would return with my oldest daughter, but she just smiled and said, "It's okay, honey. Travel safely." She didn't insist I see her again before leaving. This the same mother who before would have demanded seeing me again before leaving. I think she knew this was the last time she would bid farewell to her oldest daughter.

It was only twelve days after I had returned to America. I was retiring to bed when I was startled by the ringing of the phone. I picked up the receiver and could hear the sad voice of my older brother saying, "Mother passed away today at noon. She's free from all that pain and with God now, so try not to take it too hard." When I hung up the phone, I felt an immediate sense of relief. Yes, I was indeed thankful that Mother had finally been freed from that incredible pain. I gave thanks to God and then slept more peacefully than I had slept in a long time.

Starting the next day, however, I found myself falling into a deep state of despondency. Tears gushed down my cheeks with each thought that Mother was nowhere to be found in this world. I bawled like a baby. If I had stayed just another twelve days, I could have been with her in her final moments, and I could have gone to her funeral. I was overwhelmed with such regrets and spent countless hours thinking about her. My eyes were constantly swollen with tears.

Though Mother's six children are now geographically separated, four in America and only two in Korea, all are doing well. She deserved to be treated like a queen by us, but the reality was that she was no longer with us. And now Father has left us as well. We rushed to his side, but he had already lost consciousness, though he did momentarily regain consciousness long enough to see his sons, daughters, and sons-and daughters-in-law sitting around him before closing his eyes again forever.

And so Father was buried beside Mother, fourteen years after Mother's death. I was able to see Mother's casket when they broke ground to bury Father with her. It was as if she was with me in life again. I faced her casket and apologetically said, "I couldn't be with you in your final moments, but I'm here now, Mother. The 6-month-old granddaughter you held in your arms 33 years ago is now the mother of three fine children. After tonight I'll free my head of all the sad memories of you in pain, Mother. And, instead, I'll treasure only pleasant memories of the happy times when you were healthy and showing your brilliant smile. My beloved Mother! Can I not see you just once again, even in my dreams? Oh, Mother! I miss you so much."

Translation : Daniel Wessling

골프장에서의 행복

Bliss on the Golf Course

파아란 하늘엔 흰구름이 뭉게뭉게 피어나 있고 약간의 추위를 동반한 바람이 조금 세차다고 느낄 만큼 불어주는 오후 한때다. 모처럼 친구끼리 골프를 치자고 약속한 날이다.

정다운 얼굴들이 웃음 가득 싣고 무거운 골프백을 메고 같은 장소로 모여온다. 오랜만에 만났으니 얘깃거리가 얼마나 많은가.

S 티업이 너무 더뎌 우리는 잠시 쉬면서 가까이에 있는 연못가에 눈길을 돌렸다.

거기엔 목이 유난히 길고 키가 껑충한 날씬한 새 한마리가 회색빛으로 온몸을 치장하고 꺾어질 것 같은 가는 한 다리를 숨겨놓은채 우아한 자태를 뽐내고 있었다.

그 새 이름을 정확히 알 수는 없었지만 그 새는 분명 짝을 잃고 외로움을 달래듯 이곳저곳을 찾는 가엾은 새인것 같다. 한쪽에선 다람쥐들이 이리저리 뛰어다니며 두툼한 꼬리를 잽싸게 흔들며 신나게 움직이며 무엇인가 열심히 양 손에 쥐고 오물대기도 한다.

이곳에는 어느 골프장이나 구스가 많은데 이른 봄에는 어미 구스가 알을 낳아 준비하는 아내를 해칠까 경계하며 망을 보고 드디어 예쁜 새끼들이 하나 둘 탄생되면 누구하나 다칠세라 앞서거니 뒤서거니 보호하며 한 가족이 이 초장에서 저 초장으로 맛있는 먹이를 찾으며 나들이 하는 것을 쉽게 볼 수 있다.

동물의 세계도 자식을 사랑하고 아끼는 마음이 인간들과 조금도 다를 바 없다. 이름모를 새들이 예쁜소리를 내며 푸른 창공을 높이 나는 새도 있고 낮게 날며 자주 나뭇가지를 옮겨 다니며 부지런히 날개짓을 쳐대는 새들도 많다.

어떤 새는 온몸이 온통 까만 비단같은데 유독 날개 쪽지면에 빨간색 물감으로 동그랗게 칠해 놓은 듯한 예쁜새도 있다.

우연히 연못속을 들여다보니 조그마한 송사리떼가 꼬리를 흔들며 춤을 추듯 분주히 움직인다. 연못가엔 갈대나무 줄기들이 빙 둘러 담장을 쳐 놓은듯하고 물 한가운데에는 하늘의 뭉게 구름들을 온통 옮겨 놓은 듯 물위에도 똑같은 한폭의 그림이 있다.

나는 이곳이 지상의 천국이라 큰 소리치고 싶다.

하나님이 지은 자연의 신비스러움에 푹 빠져 있는데 내 차례란다. 티샷을 했다.

드라이버가 내 공을 정확히 맞췄다. 공은 저편 하늘을 향하여 멋있게 날아갔다.

'장타'다. 오랜만에 골프장에 나와 맛보는 황홀한 순간이다. 그러나 매번 잘 맞아주는 것은 아니다. 모두들 '오잘 공'이라고 소리친다.

'오잘공'이란 '오늘 제일 잘 친공'이란 뜻이 담긴 순수한 한국말의 준말이다.

거의 골프가 끝나가는 마지막 18번홀에서 우리는 골프를 치다말고 가까이에 있는 연못 한 가운데에서 너무나도 멋지고 근사한 퍼레이드가 순간 펼쳐지고 있는 것을 목격했다.

나와 친구 셋이만 보기에는 너무나도 아까운 퍼레이드 순간이다. 우리는 넋을 잃은 듯 한참 쳐다보았다. 맨 앞에 엄마 구스 그리고 일열로 나란히 막내딸, 막내아들 순으로 차례로 여섯 마리의 아기구스들이 적당한 거리를 맞춰 작은 엉덩이를 흔들며 엄마를 따르고 맨 뒤에는 아빠구스가 여유있게 헤엄치며 이 동네서 저 동네로 소풍을 나선 것 같았다. 비디오 카메라가 없는 것이 안타까울 정도로 아름다운 풍경이었다. 아마도 이 작품이 경연대회에 나갔으면 「가족 나들이」란 제목으로 틀림없이 일등을 차지했을 것이다.

오늘은 친구들과 골프도 즐거웠지만 하나님께서 창조하신 아름다운 자연속에서 살아 숨쉬며 건강한 몸으로 움직일 수 있도록 모든 여건을 허락하신 하나님께 감사하며 차에 시동을 건다.

가족이 있는 내 집을 향하여 차가 움직이며 천천히 골프장을 벗어나고 있다.

It was one of those afternoons with towering masses of white clouds gathering in the blue sky above. There was a somewhat aggressive wind blowing, which was accompanied by just a tinge of coolness. I was meeting up with friends for a round of golf for the first time in a long while. Affectionate faces beamed with smiles from one ear to the other as we gathered at our agreed spot, each of us shouldering heavy bags of golf clubs. The air was quickly filled with the sound of chatter from long-separated friends catching up on times missed.

Our tee-off time was significantly delayed, so we turned our attention to a nearby pond as we waited. In the pond stood a bird, tall and slender in height and boasting an unusually long neck. He was handsomely adorned with a solid gray plumage. Standing on one leg so thin it seemed ready to snap, with the other leg tucked away out of sight, he proudly flaunted his dignified nobility. I'm not sure what species of bird he was, but he seemed so pitiable wandering to and fro in search of something, perhaps an attempt to soothe his loneliness after losing his mate. Elsewhere squirrels took pleasure in scampering about, nimbly flicking their thick, bushy tails while energetically nibbling morsels held in their claws.

All golf courses seem to have a surplus of geese, and this one was no exception. In early spring, it's not at all difficult to find male geese standing guard over mates who are preoccupied with laying eggs and making preparations for their forthcoming new family members. As the cute little baby geese hatch one by one, the parents watchfully position themselves in front and behind them, lest they should fall to harm. Then they all march off as one big family, meandering from one grassy patch to another in search of tasty snacks to consume.

The world of animals is no different from that of humans. They all know how to love and care for their offspring. There are nameless birds that sing beautiful songs; birds that soar high into the blue expanse of heaven; birds that hug the ground as they fly and birds that spend their time hopping from tree branch to tree branch with wings flapping incessantly. There are also beautiful birds cloaked with silky black feathers and tattooed with a single red circle on each wing.

Sometimes when looking into the pond, I could catch glimpses of tiny minnows darting about with rapid tail swings choreographed like dance movements. Bands of reeds seemed to form a natural perimeter around the pond. The water in center was covered with a stretch of shadows cast from the towering clouds overhead, as if the same clouds were somehow transposed to the water's surface. I exclaimed that this must be heaven on earth.

I was completely engrossed in the wonders of the nature that God had created for us. Suddenly it was my turn. I teed off. My driver hit the ball squarely. The ball cut beautifully through the air. It was a long drive. I was experiencing a brief moment of ecstasy on that golf course, the first in a long while. The great shots don't happen often. Everyone shouted, "O-jal-kong," which is abbreviated Korean golf slang for "Best shot of the day!"

As we were finishing up at the 18th hole, we had to stop and again give our attention to a nearby pond, for in the center of that pond there was a grand parade unfolding before our very eyes. What a shame only my three friends and I were there to witness this magnificent event. We were awestruck as we gazed upon the spectacle for a long while.

At the very front of the procession was the mother goose. Right behind her were six perfectly spaced baby geese wagging their little tails to maintain proper intervals. They seemed to be ordered by age, the first being the youngest female, followed by the youngest male, and so on. At the back of the line, the father goose very casually swam along as if out for a stroll through the neighborhood. It was a truly impressive scene. I lamented not having a video camera with me. Had the performance been part of a competition, it likely would have been entitled "A Family Outing." And it surely would have taken top prize.

I enjoyed sharing a round of golf with friends, but I was most thankful for God's allowing me to live, breathe, and enjoy good health to move about in the beautiful nature he created. I started my car and slowly pulled away from the golf course to head back home to my family.

Translation : Daniel Wessling

9월의 문턱에서

When September Draws Near

화씨 95도~100도를 오르내리는 폭염주의보가 내려진 무더운 날이다.

기다리는 비는 안오고 누렇게 뜬 잔디는 물을 달라고 조른다.

쇼핑센터에 잠시 들어갔다 나왔는데 차 안은 완전 사우나다. 그래도 이제 몇 주만 지나면 선선한 바람이 서서히 9월의 문턱으로 불어 주겠지.

이맘때면 큰딸이 원하는 대학에 입학허가 통지를 받고 학교 갈 준비를 할 때가 생각난다. 그때도 이렇게 찜통 날씨가 계속 되었던 8월 중순이었다.

마치 시집가는 색시 모양 이것저것 사느라고 법석을 떨며 그건 안사도 돼, 아니야 사야해 하며 말씨름을 하고, 결국은 사주면서 인심을 마냥 잃고 땀을 뻘뻘 흘리며 스테이션 왜건에 작은 냉장고, 컴퓨터, 이불, 침대시

트, 베개닛, 식기, 옷가지, 책 등을 넘치도록 꾹꾹 눌러 싣고 대학기숙사를 향해 떠나는 날, 딸은 흥분해 들떠있고 엄마 마음은 쓸쓸했다.

엄마, 아빠 곁을 떠나 독립하는 딸은 무척 좋아 보였다.

한 살림 차린 자기만의 생활이 얼마나 좋겠는가 사실은 나도 학창시절로 다시 돌아올 수만 있었으면 하는 기분이니까.

예쁘게 방을 꾸미고 점심을 함께 나눈 후 작별의 시간이 됐다. 어느새 그 큰 눈에 그렁그렁 눈물이 가득 고인 것을 숨기려고 얼굴을 돌린다. 나도 갑자기 눈이 시리기 시작했다. 차를 타고 집으로 달려오면서 주체할 수 없는 눈물이 마냥 가슴을 적신다. 남편은 위로한다면서도 눈물을 속으로 삼키는가 얼굴이 굳어있다.

4년후 작은딸이 집을 떠나 학교로 갈때도 이렇게 무더운 8월 찜통 같는 날이었다. 큰딸 때 면역이 생겼나 많이 달라진 나를 보고 움찔 놀랬다.

기숙사방을 예쁘게 꾸미고 용돈도 은행계좌에 넣어 주고 돌아오는 발걸음은 그리 힘들지가 않았다.

고국으로부터 부모님이 위독하시다는 우울한 소식이 날아온 것도 9월 초! 약속이나 하신 듯 어머니도 9월 어느날, 아버지께서도 9월에 이세상을 떠나셨다. 왜 하필이면 9월인가.

내가 태어난 달도 9월이다.(음력) 고향은 평안북도 신의주, 내가 태어나던날 눈(雪) 이 얼마나 많이 왔는지 작은 키의 어른들은 눈에 파묻혀 보이지 않았다니, 그래서 할머니, 할아버지께서 나의 이름을 하얀 눈 (雪) 이라 지으셨단다. 이곳 미국에서 음력계산 하기어려워 그냥 기억하기 좋게 9월로 지키는 나의 생일날은 멀어져 가는 저편의 부모님 추억과 함께 하루를 보낸다.

작년 이맘 때 미국은 아주 평화로웠다. 누가 그 엄청난 테러가 준비되고 있는지 눈치챌 수 있었겠는가. 아침 일찍 출근해 일하고 있는데 흘러나온

뉴스, 뉴욕의 쌍둥이 빌딩에 비행기가 떨어지는 모습을 TV로 보면서 모든 사람이 치를 떨지 않았는가. 경제는 곤두박질하고 잘 나가던 회사들에 감원바람이 불고 파산하고 불경기로 여기저기서 야단들이다. 많은분들이 은퇴를 연기해야 한다니 심각하다.

9월의 문턱에 9·11 추모행사가 여기저기서 열릴 것이다. 어느 잡지 표지에서 본 갓난 아기들 얼굴로 가득 채워진 사진이 생각난다. 이 아기들이 태어나기도 전에 아빠들이 희생되었다니 얼마나 기가 막히고 슬픈 일인가. 이 아기들이 벌써 첫돌를 맞을 준비들을 하겠지. 홀어머니 밑이지만 예쁘게 잘 자라리라 믿는다. 더 이상 이 세상에 테러가 없고 평화로움이 가득하기를 기대한다.

It's a hot, steamy day with temperatures hovering between 95 and 100 degrees Fahrenheit, so hot that an excessive heat warning had to be issued. The rain we had hoped for never came. The brown grass is crying out for water. Even after just a quick stop at the shopping center, my car is already as hot as a sauna. But I know that in a few short weeks cool winds will gradually start blowing to usher in September.

This time of year, I'm reminded of when my older daughter received her acceptance letter from the school of her choice and was readying to leave for college. It was mid-August, still blistering hot like it is today. That day she was like a young bride-to-be, bustling about, buying this and buying that. We quarreled about what I thought she did and didn't need. I ended up buying her everything anyway, all the while getting quite cross and perspiring profusely. Somehow we managed to stuff her small refrigerator, computer, blankets, bed sheets, pillows, tableware, clothing, books, and other odds and ends into our station wagon and headed off to her dormitory.

Though my daughter was giddy with excitement, I was sad she was leaving us. She really seemed to relish the thought of leaving her mother and father to be independent. Actually, there is much to be said about living alone with only your self to worry about. I myself wouldn't mind reliving my school days.

After arranging everything in her room to make it look nice and pretty, we ate lunch together and then found ourselves having to say goodbye. In no time, tears began forming in her big eyes. When she turned her face away to hide her tears, I felt tears welling up in my eyes, too. During the drive back home, tears flowed uncontrollably down my face and onto my shirt. My husband did his best to comfort me, but even his face was quite stiff as he fought to swallow his own tears.

Four years later, it was my younger daughter's turn to leave for college. The day she left we had the same blistering heat of August. But this time I was much different, which surprised everyone. Perhaps the experience with my older daughter had toughened me up. We arranged everything neatly in her dorm room and deposited a little spending money in her bank account. I was much more upbeat returning home that time.

It was also in early September when I received news from Korea that my mother was seriously ill. Both my mother and father passed away in September, almost as if they had planned it that way. Why of all months did it have to be September?

My birthday is also in September (by Lunar calendar). They say that on the day I was born in Sinuiju, North Pyongan Province, it snowed so much that the shorter adults couldn't see; their eyes were buried in the snow. I'm told that this is the reason my grandparents put "Sul" in my name. "Sul" is the Korean pronunciation for the Chinese character for snow. It's difficult to really follow the Lunar calendar here in America, but I find it convenient to celebrate my Lunar-calendar birthday in September, as it lets me spend my day rekindling fading memories of my deceased parents.

Last year was a particularly peaceful year here in America. Who could have guessed that such a horrific act of terror (9/11) was being planned. I left for work early in the morning and was working when I saw news reports of the planes flying into the twin towers. Everyone shuddered at the site. This threw the economy into an immediate tailspin. Thriving companies were suddenly forced to lay off workers and petition for bankruptcy. People everywhere were in trouble because of the recession. It was so serious that many of them even had to put off their retirements.

When September draws near, many memorial activities take place. I recall seeing on the cover of a magazine a picture full of faces of newborn babies. I was shocked and saddened to learn that their fathers had all been sacrificed before they were even born. I'm sure they're all ready to celebrate their first birthdays by now. They're probably being raised by grandmothers, and no doubt growing into beautiful children. I hope the world will see no more terror, and that we'll have nothing but peace instead.

Translation : Daniel Wessling

30년

Thirty Years

우연의 일치랄까 한국에서 30년. 미국에서 30년을 살았으니 금년은 유난히도 감회가 크다.

평안북도 신의주에서 태어나 8.15 직후 3살 때 어머니 손을 잡고 3·8선을 넘어온 기억이 조금은 남아있다. 초등학교 2학년 때 6.25를 겪었고 1.4 후퇴 때 부산으로 피난 가 5학년 때 서울로 수복하고 학창시절과 직장생활을 보내고 결혼했다.

첫딸을 낳고 미국에 먼저 온 남편의 초청으로 잔뜩 부푼 꿈을 안고 3살이 채 안된 딸아이의 고사리 같은 손목을 잡고 양쪽 부모형제들의 이별, 슬픈 배웅을 받으며 태평양을 건너온 지 어언 30년.

1972년 12월에 이곳에 도착하여 처음 맞는 미국의 겨울은 참으로 추웠다. 남편은 직장 가고 딸아이를 데리고 놀이터에 나가 그네를 태워주며 밀어닥치는 향수병이 날씨만큼이나 매섭게 추워 얼마나 많이 울었는지.

머리가 까만 사람만 보면 얼마나 반가웠던지, 달려가서 한국 사람이 확인되면 금방 가까워졌다. 어느 집사님의 인도로 한국교회에 나가기 시작하면서 남편과 같이 성가대로 봉사하며 교인들과 친분을 가지며 이민생활의 즐거움을 갖기 시작했다.

미국 온 지 3개월 되는 날, 난 남편한테 구박(?)을 받으며 배운 운전으로 운전면허증을 획득했다. 그 다음날로 나이아가라, 토론토, 뉴욕으로 여행을 떠나면서 30분씩 남편과 교대로 운전을 했다. 그래야 운전이 쉽게 는다는 남편의 제의에 따라 highway에서 30분을 운전하고 나면 얼마나 긴장했던지 목이 뻣뻣하고 목돌리기가 힘들어 쩔쩔매던 잊지못할 추억이 있다.

둘째 아이를 낳아 3살이 되었을때 첫 직장을 갖게 되었다.

데이케어에 갖다 맡기고 일을 가려면 얼마나 울어대는지 함께 울었다.

이민자라면 이런 경험 안 해 본 사람이 있을까. 직장이 바쁠 땐 오버타임도 마다않고 정말 열심히 살았다.

우체국 직원이 되어 일하기도 했다.

오후 3시~11시까지 저녁 일을 2년 넘게 하다보니 산다는 것이 무엇인가 회의가 생기기 시작했다. 일 갔다 귀가하면 남편과 아이들은 곤히 잠들어있다. 늦은 저녁 먹고 금방 잘 수 없으니 TV를 보다 새벽에 잠들고, 깨면 남편은 직장으로 아이들은 학교로 텅 빈 집안에 언제나 환한 낮에는 나 혼자다.

저녁을 준비해놓고 남편과 두 딸에게 저녁 메뉴 편지를 써놓고 직장을 간다.

벌써부터 그만두라는 남편의 제의를 무시하고 이러기를 2년 8개월, 곰

곰 생각하면서 삶의 우선 순위가 무엇인가 점검해보기 시작했다.

아이들이 얼마후면 대학에 갈텐데 남편과 딸들과 함께 오손도손 저녁을 같이 먹으며 보내는 시간이 얼마나 남았나, 얼마나 중요한가를 생각해보니 용기가 생겼다.

낮 직장을 구했다. 남편이 좋아하고 두 딸이 좋아하니 마음에 평화가 찾아왔다. 미국생활 30년을 지내는 동안 한국의 형제, 친척들이 하나 둘 건너와 점점 대가족으로 늘고 있다. 딸들이 엄마의 미국생활 30년을 뜻깊은 해로 생각해 조촐한 잔치를 마련해줬다.

한때는 아이들이 성장해 결혼하고나면 한국으로 나가 살리라 잔뜩 마음 먹었었는데 점점 살면서 미국에 깊은 정이 들어가면서 정말 살 맛 나는 나라라는 마음이굳어졌다.

9·11 테러, 스나이퍼, 이런 불안, 공포가 사라지고 평화로움이 다시 이 땅에 찾아와 정말 살 맛 나는 이곳 미국에서 또 다른 30년을 건강하게 살며 수많은 아름다운 추억을 남기고 싶다.

Could it be just a coincidence that this particularly meaningful year marks the point at which I have lived a full thirty years in Korea and thirty years in America? I was born in the city of Sinuiju in North Pyongan Province. I vaguely recollect holding my mother's hand as we crossed the 38th parallel immediately after the 15 August Liberation (from Japanese colonial rule). In second grade, I experienced the June 25th outbreak of the Korean War, as well as the 4 January Retreat (due to the Chinese intervention), which forced us to seek refuge in the Pusan area. In fifth grade, I returned to Seoul, where I finished my education, worked my first job, and eventually married.

Somehow another thirty years has passed since, after giving birth to my first daughter, I endured that tearful send-off from my parents, siblings and in-laws, and then, holding the darling little hand of my not yet three-year-old daughter, full of hopes and dreams, I crossed the Pacific to be with my husband, who had emigrated first to make the arrangements for our transition.

When I arrived in December 1972, I found my first winter in America to be a bitterly cold one. While my husband was gone to work, I would take my daughter out for swings at the local playground, where being overwhelmed with homesickness as cold as winter itself, I would cry a river of tears. Whenever I'd see someone with black hair, I'd get all excited, and if that person turned out to be Korean, we'd immediately form a close bond with each other. It wasn't until I responded to someone's invitation to visit a local Korean church, where my husband and I ended up singing in the choir and becoming closely acquainted with the church members, that I was able to find any joy living life as an immigrant.

Three months after arriving in America - to the day, I endured the challenge of my husband's driving instructions and obtained my driver's license. The very next day, my husband and I departed on a road trip to Niagra Falls, Toronto, and New York. We swapped driving duties every thirty minutes, as my husband believed that this was the easiest way to get me comfortable driving. I played along, but I will never forget how frightened and tense I was after thirty minutes of highway driving. My neck was so stiff I could hardly turn my head.

I later gave birth to my second daughter and started my first job in America when she was three years old. Whenever I dropped her off at daycare on the way to work, she would cry so much that I'd find myself crying with her. But what immigrant hasn't gone through the same thing? We really worked hard. When business was good, I wouldn't decline offers for overtime work. I even worked a stint as a post office employee.

After working an evening schedule from 3:00 to 11:00 for over two years, I began to question whether this was really what life was all about. By the time I returned home from work, my husband and children would already be sound asleep. Moreover, I couldn't sleep right after eating a late dinner, so I would fall asleep watching television in the early morning hours. When I awoke the next day, my husband would be at work and the children already gone to school, leaving me alone in an empty house in the middle of the day. I would prepare my own dinner, write out a 'dinner menu' for my husband and two daughters, and then head off to work again.

For some time I had been ignoring my husband's prodding to quit my job, and life went on like this for two years and eight months. At some point I began to deeply ponder what exactly was most important in life. It wouldn't be long before the children would head off to college. How many more days would I have to sit and enjoy a nice dinner together with my husband and daughters? I thought about how important this was too me and finally found the courage to take the plunge, I quit my day job. Both my husband and two daughters were much happier for it, which brought peace to my heart.

During my thirty years in America, my siblings and relatives have made their own journeys across the Pacific, one by one forming a large, extended family here in America. Recognizing the significance of the 'thirtieth year', my daughters arranged a nice little celebration for me. There was a time when I was certain I would return to life in Korea after my children were grown and married, but not any more. Over time I have learned to love and appreciate what a wonderful country America is to live in. I just pray that the fear and anxiety resulting from the 9/11 terrorist attacks and D.C. sniper attacks will be replaced by a newfound peace in this land, and that I will be blessed with good health to live another thirty wonderful years, so that I can create many more beautiful memories of life in America, a truly incredible country to live in.

Translation : Daniel Wessling

전쟁 중의 아이들이 떠올리는 유년의 나

Children in War -- Thoughts of My Own Childhood

이라크의 전쟁을 보면서 어렸을 때 겪었던 6.25 전쟁 기억이 살아난다.

초등학교 2학년 무렵 등교하자마자 사이렌이 요란하게 울렸다. 담임 선생님이 급한 목소리로 집으로 빨리들 돌아가라고 했다.

우르르 교실 밖으로 나온 아이들은 운동장에 낯선 군복을 입은 사람들이 총대를 들고 왔다갔다하고 누가 흘렸는지 피가 낭자함을 보고 놀라 걸음아 나 살려라 숨을 헐떡거리며 단숨에 집으로 뛰어들었다.

얼마 후 아버지가 인민군에 잡혀 끌려가다가 가까스로 도망쳤으나 다시 붙잡혀 총살직전에 극적으로 살아오셨다. 이북이 고향인 아버지는 전쟁 중에 그래도 형제들과 같이 있어야 한다며 이웃도 모르게 한밤중에 식구들을 데리고 후암동 작은 집으로 옮겨가 삼형제 대가족이 함께 살았다.

아버지와 작은 아버지는 적산 가옥인 다다미를 들추고 반 지하에 들어가 숨어 지내고, 엄마와 작은 엄마는 남대문시장으로 장사를 나가 쌀, 감자 등 식량을 구해오곤 하셨다. 오빠와 나, 동생, 사촌 동생은 하루 종일 방안에서 술래잡기, 소꿉장난을 하며 재미있게 시간을 보내고, 그래도 내가 큰 언니라고 8살인 나이에 동생에게 밥을 챙겨 먹이고 오빠와 밀을 맷돌에 갈아 밀가루를 만드는 일도 잘 했다.

오빠가 소리 친다. 밖을 내다보라고. 비행기가 지나가면서 어른 팔뚝만한 검은 물체를 뚝뚝 떨어뜨리고 간다. 잠시 후 펑 소리와 함께 검은 연기와 불길이 솟아 오르는데도 그렇게 무섭지가 않았다.

어느 날 모처럼 하얀 쌀밥과 고기국으로 온 가족이 아침식사를 하는데 갑자기 쿵 소리를 내면서 온통 먼지가 쏟아지며 문짝이 넘어가고 아수라장이 됐다.

가까운 곳에 방공호가 있었는데 들락날락하는 사람을 보고 폭탄을 내려친 것이다.

집 근처에는 다리에 폭격을 맞아 너덜너덜 피를 흘리며 어디론가 울부짖으며 업혀가던 이웃 아저씨, 도망가다 총에 맞아 죽어가며 같은 동포끼린데 물 한 모금 달라고 애원하다 죽은 인민군 장교, 그리고 폭격에 죽은 많은 시신이 가마니에 쌓여 있는 것을 무수히 보았다.

얼마 후 우린 한강 다리가 끊긴 후에 영등포역 까지 걸어가 마지막으로 떠나는 짐을 가득 실은 기차 위에 올라 탔다. 좁은 공간에서 밟혀 죽은 아기를 끈을 매어 기차 밑으로 내려놓고 떠나는 어머니의 매정함이며, 터널을 지나다 떨어져 죽은 사람들, 이런 아수라장 속에서도 기차가 예고없이 설 때면 배고픔을 덜기 위해 부지런히 어른들은 기차 밑으로 내려가 떡이며 김밥을 사서 아이들에게 먹였다.

살 얼음이 언 추운날, 잠은 안 오고 초롱초롱 반짝이는 별을 세면서 촉

축히 내린 이슬에 젖은 이불을 덮고 별 하나 나 하나를 세며 짠 고등어를 먹어 목이 말라 밤새도록 얼음을 캐서 먹던 어린 피난시절을 잊지 못한다.

교회 주선으로 피난민에게 주어진 공터에 판자집을 짓고 그래도 3 년이란 세월을 피난민 학교를 다니면서 '서울내기 다마내기' 소리를 들으며 생활했던 초등학교 어린시절들이 즐거웠고, 나에게 많은 추억과 부할 때와 빈곤할 때에 맞추어 살아 가는 방법을 배운 그리 슬프지 않은 시간들이었다.

지금 이라크 전쟁 중의 아이들이 아마도 나의 어린 피난 시절과 같을 것이다. TV 뉴스와 신문을 보노라면 눈이 유난히 큰 아이가 겁에 질려 서 있는 모습이 꼭 옛날 나를 보는 것 같아 마음이 아프다.

세월이 많이 흐른 후이지만 전쟁의 기억을 떠올려 보면 어른들은 모두 슬프고 힘들어했는데도 아이들은 그렇게 슬프지 않고 오히려 더 재미 있어 하며 뛰놀았던 옛날의 기억이 생생하다. 아마도 현실을 초월한 동심의 세계에서만 가능한 것이리라. 헌데 TV 속의 이라크 어린이는 그런 동심마저도 전쟁의 참화에 빼앗겨 버린 듯 그 큰 눈의 촛점에 슬픔이 배어 있는 것 같아 안타깝기만 하다. <조선문학 수필신인상 당선작품>

As I view images of the war in Iraq, I am reminded of my own childhood experiences during the Korean War. I believe I was in the second grade at the time. The sirens sounded just after we had arrived at school. Speaking with a great sense of urgency, our teacher told us all to return home immediately. As we stampeded out of the classroom onto the playground, we saw armed soldiers clothed in strange uniforms walking about with guns. I don't know whose blood it was, but I was shocked when I saw pools of someone's blood. Urging my feet forward while gasping for air and thinking, "Spare me, dear Lord," I ran straight home in what seemed a single breath.

A little later my father was captured by the Korean People's Army (KPA) of the North. He was caught again when he attempted to flee, but just as they were readying to shoot him, he managed a dramatic escape. Being from the North himself, my father emphasized how siblings had to stick together. So, in the middle of the night, and without a word to anyone in the neighborhood, he led us all to a small house in Huamdong, where we and the families of two other siblings lived together as one large, extended family.

My father and uncle hid half underground beneath a Japanese tatami floor mat while my mother and aunt went to the Namdaemun Market to buy rice, potatoes, and other food items. I spent the whole day having fun playing tag and playing house with my older brother, younger brother, and cousin, but I also had work to do. Being the older sister, I made meals for my younger brother, and I also helped my older brother grind wheat into flour on a millstone. My brother shouted to look out the window. A war plane passing overhead dropped some black objects that looked the size of a grown man's forearm. Then we heard a big 'boom' and saw clouds of black smoke and fire billow into the air, but it didn't really scare us much.

One day our whole family was enjoying a breakfast of white rice and meat soup, the first meat in a long time, when suddenly there was a loud bang. Dust was thrown everywhere and the door fell down. The whole place was in shambles. Judging from the way people were running in and out of a nearby bomb shelter, we surmised that a bomb had been dropped. Not far from our house, a man whose leg had been hit by the blast was screaming and bleeding profusely as he was carried off somewhere on someone's back. There was a KPA officer who, having been shot while running away, died before other fellow Koreans who refused him the cup of water he begged for. There were numerous other corpses wrapped in straw bags, all victims of the blast.

Not long afterward, after the Han River Bridge had been severed, we walked to the Yeong Deung Po Station and managed to board the last train, which was heavily loaded with baggage. There I saw the heartlessness of a mother who had abandoned her baby by lowering it by a cord to a spot under the train. The baby had been trampled to death in the tight spaces. I also saw people killed when knocked off the train as it passed through a tunnel. Even amidst all this chaos, each time the train would stop without warning, the adults would agilely work their way down from the train to buy rice cakes and seaweed rice rolls to feed to their children. How could I ever forget my time as a young refugee, and those cold nights when, unable to sleep, I would cover myself with a dew-dampened blanket and count the twinkling stars one by one as I ate salty mackerel and chewed on ice all night to quench my thirst?

The refugees were given small plots of land on which a church generously built little shacks for us, which we called home for three years. However my childhood years were still happy ones, during which

I was exposed to interesting mixes of standard Seoul and regional dialects at the refugee grade school I attended. Those years left me with many memories that were not so terribly sad. And they taught me how to adjust to life in wealth and life in poverty.

I think these Iraqi children living through war today are probably experiencing much of what I did as a child refugee. It truly pains me to see in newspapers or television news broadcasts the Iraqi children with their unusually large eyes frozen in fear. I feel I am seeing myself as a child many years ago. Many years have passed, but when I recall those war years, which were so very difficult and sad for the adults, I remember how we as children were not so sad, actually. On the contrary, I have many vivid childhood memories of having fun and running around. Such things are possible only in the imaginary world of a child who can somehow manage to transcend reality. Still it hurts me to see on television how those young Iraqi children are victims of the ravages of war, and how their sadness permeates their young eyes.

<Winner of the Chosun Literature New Essayist Award>

Translation : Daniel Wessling

기(氣)의 고장 세도나

Sedona: The Land of Energy

캘리포니아의 끝없이 이어지는 대륙의 사막을 달려 콜로라도 강을 건너자마자 네바다 주에서 애리조나 주로 바뀌었다. 뾰족뾰족한 가시들을 온몸에 박아놓고 도도하게 자태를 뽐내는 형형 각색의 선인장들, 울퉁불퉁한 붉은 돌멩이와 붉은 흙으로 뒤덮인 광활한 사막을 바라보며 감상을 하자니 순간 '아리조나 카우보이' 노래가 절로 흥얼거려진다.

노랗게 물든 단풍잎들을 매단 거무튀튀한 나무들과 곁에 어우러져 있는 큰 웅덩이, 바로 사막 속에 오아시스가 아닌가? 웅덩이에 고여있는 짙푸른 물이 불어오는 바람에 물결을 만든다. 시커먼 구름 사이에 붉은 태양이 얼굴을 내미는가 했더니 갑자기 쏟아지는 눈보라가 심술 부리며 시야를 방해한다. 사막 저편에 길게 누워있는 기차길, 그 철로 위에 끝이 보이지 않는 긴 행렬의 적재차가 마치 구렁이같이 철길을 따라 느긋하게 기어가고 있다.

세도나로 가는 길목에 신 아구아(Sin Agua)라는 인디언들이 살다 떠나 버린 신비의 검은 호두나무 계곡 속은 아늑하기만 하다. 가파른 절벽 바위 틈에 지혜롭게 지어놓은 동굴을 들여다보니 그들 특유의 소리를 꽥꽥 질러대며 울긋불긋한 옷을 입은 인디언들이 마구 뛰어나올것 같은 오싹함을 느꼈다.

슬라이드 락 주립공원의 잘 다듬어진 그림 같은 골짜기를 따라 하얀 거품을 일구며 흐르는 얼음장같이 시린 계곡물에 온몸을 담근 모험심 강한 백인 청년들의 기막힌 인내심, 온몸의 기를 받기 위해서라니, 믿기는 어려웠지만 벌벌 떠는 모습이 애처롭기도 했다.

드디어 구름 한 점도 없는 맑은 하늘, 온통 붉게 물든 사막, 불모지 땅을 뚫고 솟아오른 붉은 산들이 병풍처럼 눈에 들어온다. 애리조나 주 북쪽 사막에 위치한 기의 고장 세도나는 미 개척시대 인디언들의 성지로 그들의 전설 속에선 영원한 생명을 주는 어머니의 에너지가 나오는 것으로 알려져 있다.

지난 해 USA 투데이가 선정한 미국 내에서 가장 아름다운 10곳 중 1위를 차지한 곳이지만 세계 각국의 명상가 사이에서는 보텍스(Vortex: 지구 내부에서 방대한 에너지가 분출되거나 우주로부터 에너지가 들어 오는 곳)로 불리는 신비로운 기운이 넘쳐나는 것으로 유명하다.

명상가들에 따르면, 세도나는 전 세계 21개 보텍스 중 5개가 집중되어 있는 명당으로 해마다 우주의 기를 받기 위해 수많은 사람들, 명상가들, 관광객들의 발길이 끊이지 않는단다.

특히 이번 여행의 하이라이트는 땅속에서 하늘로 기가 솟아오른다는 종 바위(bellrock)와 우주의 기가 땅위로 모인다는 대성당 바위(cathedral rock)에 올라 기(氣)를 체험하는 것이다.

손발에 전기가 오는 듯 짜릿한 파동을 느끼며 정말 기를 받는 것일까? 어리둥절하기도 하고 여기저기서 환호성이 터진다.

45일간의 긴 여행길에도 피곤하지 않고 개운함은 아마도 세도나의 기(氣) 덕을 본 것일까, 그렇다면 이번 여행은 큰 수확이다.

자연의 숭고한 기(氣)의 고장 세도나는 오묘하고 온통 붉음의 신비로움을 안고 마음 설레게 하는곳, 하나님께서 지으신 대자연에 감탄하며 자연은 언제나 인간 앞에 진실하게 훈훈하고 정겹게 살아가라는 교훈을 주는 것 같다. 그래서 우리가 자연을 찾아가는 것보다 자연이 우리를 한없이 기다려 주는 지도 모른다. <해외문학 수필 신인상 당선작품>

East, driving past the deserts of California and across the Colorado River, I arrive at the Arizona state line. With prickly spines, standing tall, in every color and form, the cacti are abundant and the various shapes of red sandstone formations and the expansive red desert makes me want to sing "The Arizona Cowboy." With dark-barked trees covered with autumn-colored leaves near a deep gorge, is it not an oasis in the desert?

The deep indigo water of the gorge ripples as a breeze comes through. While the crimson sun emerges briefly between the dark clouds, a sudden snowstorm mischievously veils our vision. Across from the desert, an endlessly long, fully-loaded freight train slowly runs along the rail track like a serpent.

Before reaching a town called Sedona, there are ancient dwellings of the Sinagua Indians - black walnut groves, quietly calming. As I look into the skillfully carved caves along the steep cliff walls, cold chills go down my back as I imagine richly-attired natives dashing out with their war cries. While passing through the Slide Rock State Park, I see the picturesquely-foaming Slippery Creek, flowing with icy cold water. There are some adventuresome young men dipping in the cold water to soak in the energy of the land. I am in awe of their strength, though I pity their shivering.

Finally I was faced with a cloudless sky, the red-hued desert, and the red sandstone rock formations rising from the empty desert, forming a beautiful screen on the land. "The land of energy," Sedona, is located in the upper desert area of Arizona, known to the American Indians of the region as a sacred ground, giving eternal life by the Great Mother's spirit.

Sedona has been selected as one of the top ten most beautiful places in the United States by USA Today. Many New Age practitioners from around the world see it as a spiritual vortex, where mysterious energy overflows. According to them, Sedona possesses five of the twenty-one vortices of the world.

The highlights of my trip include Bell Rock, which is said to draw up energy from the center of the earth, and the Cathedral Rock, which is said to draw down the energy from the universe itself. As I sense electrical sparks through my hands and feet, I wonder if it's true. Some are even shouting for joy and feeling surprisingly disorientated.

Even after forty-five days on this long trip, I feel energized and light.

If it is due to Sedona's energy, I would say the trip was worthwhile! The land of naturally subliminal energy, Sedona makes me tremble for its uncanny and profound redness. It makes me marvel at the beauty created by God, teaching us to live truthfully, warmly, and affectionately. Therefore, it is probably better to think of nature, not as some passive place that we visit, but as a place anxiously and always awaiting us.

<Winner of the Korean Expatriate Literature New Essayist Award>

Translation : Eunhwa Choe

새 보금자리

A New Nest

나이 90세가 넘은 한 유명한 사진 작가가 있었읍니다. 어떤 사람이 그에게 물었읍니다. "당신은 지난 72년 동안 사진작가로 크게 활약을 했는데 그 많은 작품중에서 제일 마음에 드는 좋은 작품은 어느 것입니까?"

그 사진 작가는 서슴치않고 "내일 아침에 찍을 사진입니다". 라고 대답했읍니다.

그렇다. 언제든지 생각은 미래에 있어야 한다. 과거에 매어서는 안된다. 과거에 얽메어서도 안되지만 미래는 무조건 행복할것 이라는 환상에 젖어 현재를 돌보지 않은 것은 어리석은 일이다. 스스로에게 미래 지향적인 비전을 제시하고 그 목표를 위해 현재의 삶을 부지런히 돌볼 때 행복한 미래는 보장된다고 생각한다.

오래 전부터 큰 딸이 인터넷에서 자기식구에 알맞는 집을 찾는다고 매일 자투리시간을 할애하며 집 헌팅를 하더니 드디어 마음에 드는 집을 찾았단다. "엄마, 아빠 내일 오셔서 집을 한번 봐주세요." 아주 흥분된 목소리다. 결혼 후 첫 보금자리 주택을 자신들이 설계해 아담하게 지어 입주한 지 7년이 되었다.

그 동안 줄줄이 사탕으로 태어난 네 아이, 여섯 식구 대가족이 되었다. 아이들이 각방을 차지해야 하는 처지에 놓이고, 좀 큰 집의 필요성을 느끼더니 흠뻑 흥분된 목소리에 희망이 넘쳐보인다.

복덕방 아저씨가 이끄는 대로 현관문을 열고 들어가니 뻥 뚫린 천장에 화려하게 반짝거리는 샹들리에가 반겨준다. 저 켠 벽에 위치한 벽난로에서는 이글이글 타오르는 장작불에 낭만이 가득 실려있다.

딸이 말한다. "이 집의 특징은요, 매스터 베드룸이 둘이 있는 거예요" 일층에 하나 그리고 위층에 있단다. 엄마, 아빠가 점점 나이가 들어가니 언제가는 실버 타운에 들아가야 할까 봐 오르내리는 것이 힘들 때를 대비해서 엄마 아빠를 위한 방이었으면 한단다. 말만 들어도 고마운데 이런 배려까지 하고 있다니 감격스런 침묵이 흐른다. 그러나 우린 분명 집이 있고 방문할 때 기꺼이 이용할 것임을 알려준다.

계약이 성사되고 이제 이사할 일만 남았다. 딸은 벌써부터 분주하게 아이들의 방 사이즈에 맞춰 가구며 커튼에 신경을 쓰며 이제 유치원에 다니는 큰 손녀딸과 의견을 맞추곤 한다. 조용하게 앉아 있지를 못하고 언제나 깔갈거리고 활달하게 뛰노는 것이 건강한 아이들의 세계가 아닌가.

멋지게 산다는 것은 젊은 날의 꿈이다. 그러나 이 꿈은 하늘에서 두둥실 다가와 품에 안기는 것이 아니라 살아가는 세속의 틈새에서 자아의 개성을 살려내고 이 개성을 통해 자아성취의 화려한 색채와 향기가 우러나와서 이루어지는 것이다.

언제나 웃으며 바라보는 아이들과 한결같이 자신의 울타리 안에서 사는 혈연이라는 끊을 수 없는 밧줄로 묶여져 살아가야 한다는 삶의 의미이며, 부모의 역활은 끊임없는 사랑과 관심을 보여주는 것이다. 모든 일에 적극적이고 긍정적인 자세로 살아가면 아이들은 부모가 모르는 사이에 성숙하고, 슬기롭고, 강인하게 잘 자랄 것이다.

보다 나은 내일을 향해 새 보금자리에서 정녕 생기있고 , 화목하고, 보람된 삶이 펼쳐지기를 바라는 마음이다.

There was a famous photographer who was in his nineties. A man asked him, "What picture do you like best among your work over the past seventy two years?" The photographer answered without hesitation "the picture I will take tomorrow."

Well, we have to think about the future. We cannot dwell in the past. We cannot have an illusion that the future will be happy and secure, so that we don't live our present lives to the fullest. This is silly. If we have some goal and vision for the future and live our present lives faithfully, our happiness will follow.

My older daughter was looking for a house on the internet for a while and has found one. One day she called on the phone and said "Mom and Dad, please come and look at the house." Her voice was full of excitement. After they got married they designed and built the house they now live in, which was seven years ago. They had baby after baby almost every year and are now at four. There are six in their family, a big family by today's standards. The children needed their own rooms and the house got too small.

The real estate agent led us to the new house. There was a high ceiling and a chandelier when we entered. The fireplace greeted us with warmth and comfort. My daughter tells me the special feature of this house is that it has two master bedrooms. One is on the first floor, the other on the second. She said that Mom and Dad can live in the one on the first floor when they are older. I was touched by her sweet thought. I told her we have our home now but we'll use the room when we visit.

All the papers went through well and the moving chore remains. My daughter is busy buying furniture and getting curtains for windows. She consults her eldest daughter who is in kindergarten asking her what color she would like for her room. The kids cannot sit still. They always move and jump.

We all dream of living well in a beautiful house and having happy kids, but this happiness doesn't drop from the sky. We have to work for it. As parents and children, we live near an invisible boundary line. The role of parents is always to show our children love and support in their decisions and to also give them courage and encouragement so that they will become mature and wise adults.

I hope and pray for a better future for them in their now-spacious nest.

Translation : Young Cha Son (Lee)

뽀삐와의 추억

Remembering Bopey

뽀삐와 인연을 맺은것은 14년 전 1992년 늦은 봄이다. 늘 즐거움을 주던 작은딸마저 대학에 가고 보니 갑자기 적막강산이 된 듯 외로움이 밀려왔다.

"언니 강아지 한 마리가 생겼는데 길러보지 않겠어?" 어느 날 동생의 전화다. 난 잠시 망설이면서 "그래, 내가 길러 볼께". 황급히 동생네 집으로 달려갔다.

하얀 털을 가진 8파운드의 몸매, 둥근 공처럼 털을 깎아주지 않아 완전 털보에다 까만 눈만 빠끔 나를 응시한다. 이름은 뽀삐, 생후 1개월이란다.

강아지를 좋아하지 않던 나, 중년의 갱년기 위기를 달래듯 뽀삐를 품에 안고와 한가족이 되었다.

이발하고 목욕하고 나니 완전 움직이는 인형이다.

같은 침대에서 잔다는 건 아예 내 사전에 없었는데 어느 날부터 자연스레 한 침대에서, 어떤 때는 내 품에 안겨 잠든 모습을 보며 정이란 이렇게 무서운 거다. 꼭 내 자식 같다.

새벽이면 뽀삐를 앞세우고 산책을 나설라치면 좋아라 깡충깡충 뛰며 힐끔힐끔 나를 돌아보며 히죽 웃음 지어준다. 거짓말 한다고요? 강아지도 기분이 좋으면 웃는 것을 모르는군요. 비가 오는 날이면 방안에서 술래잡기를 한다. 나는 숨고 뽀삐는 신이나서 위층, 아래층, 지하실로 나를 찾으러 헤매다가 나와 눈이 마주치면 움칠 놀라 흑진주 같은 눈을 동그랗게 뜨고 나를 똑 바로 응시하던 즐거웠던 그 순간들!

한번은 우리 집에 도둑이 들었었다. 용감하게도 조그마한 녀석이 겁도 없이 끈질기게 악을 쓰며 짖어대어 도둑을 쫓아내 변을 면케한 기특하고 장한 뽀삐였다. 8년 전 어느 날 뽀삐의 눈에 큰 이상이 생겼다. 다행이도 눈물샘이 막힌 것을 발견, 침샘을 눈으로 연결하는 수술에 성공, 초롱초롱한 맑은 눈을 회복됐다. 얼마나 기뻤던가.

그러나 밥을 먹을 때는 침샘이 눈으로 연결되어 있어 눈물을 뚝뚝 흘리며 먹는데 얼마나 불편했을까, 곁에서 지키고 있다가 눈물을 닦아주곤 했었다. 눈 수술후에는 강한 강아지 샴푸대신 아기들 샴푸로 목욕시키고 전용미용사로 각별한 사랑을 주고 받았던 귀염둥이 나의 뽀삐. 하필이면 나의 짧은 고국나들이 동안에 나를

기다리지 못하고 떠나고 말았다.

미시간, 뉴욕, 보스턴등지로 오가며 13년반을 함께 한 수많은 추억들이 나를 이렇게 울보로 만들어 놓고 가버린 뽀삐. 온가족의 사랑을 듬뿍 받았던 뽀삐의 텅 빈 자리가 이렇게 가슴아프게 클 줄이야. 너무 안타깝구나. 언제 너를 잊을 수 있겠니. 사랑하는 뽀삐야, 정말 보고 싶다.

I have known Bopey since late Spring 1992. Our youngest daughter who gave us laughter left us to go to college and we felt the empty nest syndrome. The house was too quiet and lonely. Then one day one of my sisters called on the phone and said, "Would you like a puppy?" I hesitated for a while and then agreed to raise the puppy. I drove straight to my sister's house. There he was, an all-white furry body without grooming with big dark eyes looking at me. His name was Bopey and he was one month old. I used to not like dogs but I brought him home cautiously and we became a family. I gave him a haircut and bathed him and he became a moving doll.

I never liked the idea of sleeping with a dog, but one day it became a natural thing. I thought to myself that bonding is a fearful thing. He was like my child. Early in the morning I took him for a walk around the neighborhood. He jumped and looked, and smiled back at me. You think I am exaggerating? When a dog is happy he smiles too. On rainy days we played hide-and-seek in the house. I would hide and Bopey would run upstairs, downstairs and to the basement to look for me and when our eyes met he would look at me, startled, with his black pearl-like eyes. I have lots of fun memories of him. One time a robber came into our house. This little creature fearlessly barked at the intruder so we didn't lose anything. He was incredible.

About eight years ago he had a problem in one eye. Fortunately the vet diagnosed it well and operated on his eye. His tear duct was clogged so the vet connected his salivary gland to his tear duct. The operation was a success and his eyes once again shined. I was so happy but there was one problem. Whenever he ate tears would flow as if he were crying. I had to wipe his tears when he ate. After the surgery, I changed his regular shampoo to baby shampoo and took him to a dog groomer for a haircut.

We loved him and he gave us a lot of joy. This loving Bopey died while I was visiting Korea. He could not wait for me to come back. I was saddened when I heard the news of his passing.

During the last 13 and half years, we took him to Michigan, New York and Boston and have many fond memories. He made me a grieving mother. He was the center of attention and our whole family loved him so much. He left us a big empty space in our heart. When can we forget you? Dear Bopey, we miss you so much.

Translation : Young Cha Son (Lee)

고국 나들이

A Trip Home

매 2년마다 열리는 국제 동창회가 금년에는 서울 워커힐에서 열리게 됐다. 동창회에 참석하기 위해 쌘프란시스코에 사는 단짝 친구와 몇 개월 전부터 세밀한 계획을 세우면서 멋진 고국 나들이를 꿈꾸어 왔다.

드디어 고국 가는 비행기 한 좌석을 차지하고, 도도한 사람들의 물결 속에 섞여 어둑해지는 저녁시간에 인천 국제공항에 도착했다. 오래간만에 반가운 형제들간의 정겨운 만남! 짧은 일정에 따라 하루하루 바빠지기 시작했다.

워커힐 비스타 홀에서 개교 60주년 기념 및 총 동문회의 밤이 열렸다. 선후배 930여명이 모이는 대대적인 뜻깊은 행사와 여흥시간속에서도 우린 45년만에 만난 단발머리 시절의 동기동창들을 바라보는 것만으로도 얼마나 즐겁고 행복했는지 모른다.

동창산악회에서 주관한 금강산 관광에 합류, 고성을 향하여 두대의 대형버스에 올랐다. 설악산을 저 켠으로 바라보며 북쪽으로 달려 비자심사 후, 오랜만에 동기동창들이 숙소인 한 펜션에서, 마침 그날은 특별한 날, 스위스와 우리나라의 축구경기가 있어 응원하느라 와, 와 소리지르며 완전 여고 때 수확여행 온 기분에 사로잡혀 온 밤을 하얗게 지새웠다.

비룡폭포, 구룡폭포를 오르느라 땀을 흠뻑 쏟고 다음날 아침부터 비가 내리는 안개 낀날, 만물상 정상까지 오르는 힘겨운 산행에 합세, 망양대 정상에 올라 V 자를 그리며 탄성의 기쁨도 맛보았다, 안개가 뿌옇게 끼였지만 오후가 되면서 구름이 서서이 아래로 내려가니 구름 위에 떠있는 것 같은 금강산 일만 이천봉의 황홀한 풍경, 골짜기마다 구름바다를 이룬 운해의 모습이 너무나 신비로웠다.

자연의 평화와는 전혀 다른 2박 3일간 금강산 주위의 표정은 우방국가와는 전혀 다른 세계, 김일성 배지의 무게(?) 만큼이랄까, 표정들이 어둡다. 말조심, 손가락 움직임 주의, 돌멩이 하나라도 등등의 가이드의 엄한 주의사항에 모두가 머쓱한 표정들이었다. 서커스는 정말 손에 땀을 쥐게 한다. 얼마나 연습을 했으면 저렇게 잘할 수 있을까 안스러운 눈물이 흐른다.

낙오자 없이 안전하게 남쪽으로 돌아왔다.

잘 꾸며진 청계천을 걸으며 징검다리를 건너보는 즐거움을 갖기도 했다. 3박 4일간 충청, 전라, 한려수도 여행에 나섰다. 첫 출발지인 서해대교를 지나며 펼쳐진 고국의 산천들…. 어디다 내놔도 뒤지지않는 우리나라의 발전된 모습을 마냥 자랑하고 싶어진다. 부산에서 KTX을 타고 서울로 2시간 45분만에 도착 했다.

50년 지기 단발머리시절의 단짝과 단둘만이 오붓하게 가져본 고국 나들이. 잊을 수 없는 순간 순간의 추억들이 내 삶의 정겨운 활력소가 되고 있다.

There is an international alumni meeting every two years. This year it will be held in Seoul at Walker Hill. I have been planning to attend the meeting for several months with my best friend from San Francisco. We had high hopes for this visit to our alma mater and for seeing old friends.

I arrived at Inchon Airport and met my siblings. It was a short trip and we were on a tight schedule. It was also the 60th birthday of our high school. The alumni meeting was held at Walker Hill in Vista Hall. It was a big event; about 930 alumni came from all over the world. We saw friends we had not seen for 45 years, since we were teenagers.

There is an alpinist club among alumni and they organized a trip to Kum Kang San (mountain). Two buses full of alumni drove east along the countryside to bypass the Sul Ak San checkpoint. We left South Korea and entered North Korea after a short visa check. We were assigned to a pension which was our home for the next two days. That day was special because Korea and Switzerland were playing in the World Cup soccer game. We were all excited and were in high spirits like school girls on a field trip. We climbed BiYoung Falls and Nine Dragon Falls and worked up a sweat.

Next morning it was soggy because of fog. We braved the misty fog and climbed to the top of Man Mul Sang and made "V"s with our fingers when we conquered the top ("mangyandae"). It was foggy but sometimes clear enough so we could see the beautiful shapes of rocks and scenery below us. All the fog, cloud and sun makes Kum Kang San a mystical place that draws many people back. It is a beautiful and serene place but people from North Korea were wearing Kim Il Sung badges and were very solemn. We were instructed to be careful about pointing with fingers and not making political remarks. We were guests visiting to enjoy the mountain. The circus performance was very thrilling. How much practice do they do to perfect the show? It made me feel very sad. We all came out without incidence.

Back in Seoul we walked Chung Kae Chun which is well landscaped and clean. We crossed the stream by stepping on a stone pass. We booked another trip for 3 days to the southern peninsula. We visited Chung Cheng and Chunla province and visited Hansando Island.

In South Korea, the infrastructure is well established and it is a very modern, beautiful country that I am proud of. From Pusan we took the KTX train and arrived in Seoul in 2 hours and 45 minutes. The visit home with childhood friends of fifty years was very memorable and gave me new energy for life.

Translation : Young Cha Son (Lee)

도레미파솔라시도의 합창

The Making of a 'Do Re Mi Fa So La Ti Do' Choir

구름발 사이로 번져오고 있는 붉은 황혼은 섬머타임으로 인하여 더 빨리 도시를 감싸더니 어둠이 다시 황혼을 잠재우며 집집마다 불빛이 하나 둘 켜지기 시작한다.

남편과 나는 큰 딸네 집을 나와 어둠을 뚫고 하이웨이를 마구 달려온다.

어제는 할로윈데이라 어린 손주들의 둘러리로 점잖은 할아버지가 다리가 아프도록 이웃 문전을 함께 기웃거리며 캔디를 얻는 아름답고 열린 기억의 사진첩을 엮는 역할이 혈연이라는 끊을 수 없는 밧줄이었기에 가능한 것이리라.

조용하게 앉아 있지를 못하고 떠들고 뛰는것이 아이들의 세계다.

할로윈 캔디 주머니에 얻어온 많은 캔디를 꺼내놓고 깔깔거리며 떠들고

먹으며 신나하는 모습들을 디지털 카메라로 귀여운 장면을 담느라고 어른들은 정신이 없다 .끊임없는 사랑과 관심을 보여주며 적극적이고 긍정적인 자세를 보이는 것이 부모의 역할이 아닌가.

또 요즘 아이들은 옛날 우리가 자랄 때와는 영 다르다. 세살이 채 안된 아이들도 컴퓨터 게임을 혼자 작동하며 머뭇거리지 않고 솔직하고 대담하게 자기표현도 잘 하는 아이들을 바라보노라면 깜짝 놀라기도 한다.

갓 태어난 아기의 울움소리가 우렁차다.

1972년에 미국 땅을 밟은 이민 초기 어렵게 생활전선에서 뛰느라 딸 둘로 만족해야만 했던 그 힘든 시절, 나의 딸들은 언니, 동생으로 만은 무척 외로웠었나보다. 그런 이유였나? 결혼후 딸들이 경쟁을 하듯 2002년에는 하루 차이로 손자, 손녀를 낳더니 이번에는 열 하루 차이로 손녀, 손자를 낳아 엄마를 엄청 긴장시키며 조바심을 내게 했으니 말이다.

큰 손녀의 나이가 3개월 모자라는 7살로 시작해서 생후 1개월의 갓난아기로 큰 딸이 다섯, 작은 딸이 셋 줄줄이 8명의 손자, 손녀를 갖게 된 할머니, 정말 손주복이 터졌다. 멀리 미시간에 가서 3주간 해산간호를 허리 휘청거리도록 하고 돌아와서는 곧바로 큰 딸네로 달려가느라 얼마나 바빴는지 모른다.

그러나 생명은 신비 속에 존재하는 것이니 건강함속에서 태어났으니 한

없는 하나님의 사랑에 감사하며 고맙고 넘치게 행복함을 느낀다. 그리고 희망도 존재함을 안다.

맑고 드높고 뭉게뭉게 흰솜털 구름이 잔잔히 펼쳐진 가을하늘을 본다.

자라나는 아이들의 머리를 얼마나 쓰다듬었는가에 따라 어린것이 바른 생활의 꽃이 피는 것, 그것은 정성의 손끝이다. 자라나는 아이들이 안정되고 변화없는 질서 속에서 파릇한 새싹를 키우며 순진하고 천진난만한 어린이들일지라도 수가 많으면 많은 파워가 생기는 법일게다.

도레미파솔라시도의 네 손자, 네 손녀. 여덟 명의 손주들이 머리가 크고 키가 자라 건강함속에서 서로서로에게 감사하며 우애있게 서로 도우며 성장하기를 바라는 마음이다. 내 주위의 많은 분들이 딸 둘에서 손주가 여덟 명이라고 하면 모두 어머나 ! 왜? 그렇게 많이 낳아요? 하고 놀란다. 그러면 나의 대답은 합창단을 만든데요 다.

꽃들이 그 만큼 빗줄기에 두들겨 맞으면서도 꽃들은 온전히 제 모양을 갖추고 있어서 꽃잎 하나 흩트러진게 없듯이 어떤 어려움이 와도 '고통은 인내를 낳고 인내는 시련을 이겨내는 끈기를 낳고 그러한 끈기는 희망을 낳는다' 라고 한 성경의 말씀대로 바르게 성장하면서 겸손하고 성실하게 자기성장과 충족을 가질 수 있는 각자 각자의 밝고 정확한 자기 적성에 맞는 확실한 음을 내는 도레미파솔라시도의 멋진 합창소리가 듣고 싶은 간절한 소원을 벌써부터 해보게되니 욕심이 과한 것일까.

The clocks now set back an hour, red rays of twilight more hastily expand through the cloud base to swathe the city below, only to be swiftly lulled to sleep by darkness, triggering a succession of lights igniting in all the houses below. My husband and I slip away from our daughter's house, slashing through the darkness of the highway.

Yesterday was Halloween. Only unbreakable blood ties made possible the building of a photo album with such beautiful, naive memories of a cultured grandfather childishly peeping into doorways to receive alms of candy, legs aching as he escorts his young grandchildren through the neighborhood.

Children can't sit still. Isn't theirs a world of running around and being loud and boisterous? Parents engross themselves in memorializing adorable scenes of euphoric children exuberantly screaming with laughter while indulging themselves with Halloween candy retrieved from overstuffed pockets. Isn't it the parents' role to give their children constant love and attention, and to continually demonstrate a positive and cheerful attitude?

Clearly these children are not like the children we once were. I am utterly amazed when I see children not yet years old effortlessly commanding computer games unassisted, and at how well they express themselves, so bold and unpretentious.

The crying of a newborn baby fills the air. It was 1972 when I first stepped on American soil. It was a difficult time, a time when we were busy struggling in the battle of life. We had to be content with just two daughters. They seemed so lonely with just one sibling to turn to. Or was it something else?

After marrying, my two daughters seemed to be engaged in a fertility competition. Both gave birth to babies within a day of each other in 2002, a boy followed by a girl. Later they gave birth within just eleven days of each other, this time a girl and then a boy, which really left me stressed and anxious.

One can imagine how busy I am now with eight grandchildren, five belonging to my oldest daughter, three to my youngest, all close in age, starting with the oldest being three months shy of seven and the youngest just a month old.

I have truly been blessed with grandchildren. But I've also been extremely busy traveling far to Michigan to provide backbreaking post-childbirth care for three weeks, after which I had to run straight to my oldest daughter's house. But life is wrapped in mystery, and I've been blessed with good health, so I'm just thankful for and overjoyed with God's boundless love. And I know there is always hope.

The autumn sky is high and clear. Thick, white downy clouds silently roll across it. With the right amount of love in fingertips that stroke the heads of growing children, those children will blossom into upstanding citizens.

Even simple, innocent young children raised as tender sprouts in a stable, secure environment show they have great power in numbers. I want nothing but for my eight 'Do Re Mi Fa So La Ti Do' grandsons and granddaughters to grow healthy physically and mentally, always being thankful, kind, and supportive toward each other.

Many of my acquaintances are shocked when they learn I have eight grandchildren from just two daughters. They all respond with shock, saying, "Goodness gracious! Why so many children?" To which I respond, "To make their own choir."

Like flowers perfectly keeping their shape, not allowing even a broken petal, when pounded by a downpour of rain, the Bible teaches us that in any hardship suffering produces perseverance; perseverance, character; and character, hope. Am I asking for too much too soon? My fervent desire is to hear the harmonious chorus of this beautiful 'Do Re Mi Fa So La Ti Do' choir producing their wonderful music in a manner that distinctively and clearly reflects the precise characteristic sounds of each member, as they grow to be upright, humble, and faithful in their own ways.

Translation : Daniel Wessling

소문만복래(笑門萬福來)

Fortune Comes to a Merry Home

다사다난 했던 2006년도 멀어져가고 희망찬 정해년(丁亥年)새해가 밝았다.

매년 그래왔듯이 성탄절은 큰딸네서 온가족이 모여 아기 예수님의 탄생을 기뻐하며 즐거운 한 때를 보냈다. 유치원생인 큰손녀딸을 위시해서 아래로 올망졸망 똑같은 예쁜 빨간 드레스를 입은 4명의 손녀들, 까만바지에 빨간 티셔츠를 입은 4명의 손자들. 바라보기만 해도 흐뭇하고 정겨운 한 폭의 그림 같은 이들의 천진난만한 웃음소리에 마냥 행복에 젖는 시간이었다.

제각기 제몫의 선물 꾸러미를 안고 풀며 깡충깡충 뛰며 좋아라 함성을 지르는 아이들. 남의 선물을 제 것이라 힘겨르기로 뺏어놓고는 울어대는 동생에게 넌지시 건네며 Okay! This is yours! 하고 큰소리 쳐대는 의젓함(?), 그간 배운 발레 춤을 추어대는 손녀들, 태권도를 하는 손자는 얏, 소리를 외쳐대며 멋진 모습을 선 보인다.

더욱이 사돈내외와의 만남의 시간이 얼마나 즐거운지, 의사이며 피아니스트인 바깥사돈은 가족들의 모임엔 언제나 피아노연주로 작은 음악회를 만들어 주곤 한다. 크리스마스캐롤을 비롯해 가곡 특히나 우리나라 애국가를 연주할 때면 '동해물과 백두산이 마르고 닳토록…'을 부르며 얼마나 감사한지.

또한 알렉산드리아 시티의 부시장으로 지역사회 봉사자로 일하는 안사돈은 외아들 몸에서 딸, 아들, 딸, 아들, 딸 순으로 다섯 손주를 낳아준 며느리가 기특해 원더풀! I am proud! 를 연발하는 자상한 모습에서 행복함을 본다. 결혼은 꼭 동족이여야 한다고 했던 나 아닌가.

스텐포드 의대 윌리암 프라이 박사의 조사 결과에 따르면 6세 정도의 유치원생들은 하루 평균 300번 정도 웃는단다. 그러나 성인이 되면 그 20분의 1인 15번 정도로 줄어든다고 한다. 웃음은 몸과 마음에 도움이 되는 것, 사람과 사람을 이어주는 접착제 같은 것이 아닐까. 사람들은 왜 잘 웃는 사람들을 좋아할까. 그런 사람과 함께 있으면 덩달아 기분이 좋아지기 때문이며 그래서 웃음은 전염병과 같은 것. 미소를 보내면 역시 미소를 보내오지 않는가.

침울한 표정을 쳐다보기만 해도 기분이 쳐진다. 하지만 환하게 웃는표정을 보고만 있어도 기분이 고조된다. 만나는 것만으로도 즐거운 사람, 그리고 교만하지 않으면서도 자신감이 넘치고 당당한 사람들을 만나면 덩달아 기분이 좋아 미소가 절로 지어진다.

이제 아이들 같이 많이 웃으며 살자. 모든 면을 긍정적으로 바라보는 시선 속에 애정과 너그러움이 채워져 날마다 새로워져야 할 것이다. 언제나 부드러움 속에서 웃는 얼굴로 서로의 프라이버시를 인정하고 경계를 지키는 것은 건강한 관계의 필수요소라 생각된다.

어떤 책에서 읽은 구절이 생각난다. 이세상에서 가장 큰기쁨은 날마다 새롭다는 것이다. 해는 어제와 같이 떠오르지만 햇빛은 어제의 햇빛이 아니고 꽃은 한 나무에서 피지만 날마다 다른 모습으로 피어난다. 소문만복래(笑門萬福來). 웃는 문으로 만복이 들어온다는 말 같이 예년보다 더 성숙한 긍정적인 삶속에서 마냥 행복하게 미소 지우며 살고 싶다.

The rather eventful year of 2006 has come and gone and it is a new year. The Year of the Boar, full of hope, has brightly dawned. As we have done for many years now, we spent Christmas, the celebration of the joyful birth of Baby Jesus, at our older daughter's home. Including our oldest granddaughter, a kindergartner, there were four granddaughters of various sizes, with the same-styled red dresses, and also four grandsons with red shirts and black pants. It was a happy time filled with warmth, as we watched their innocent laughter.

The children gathered their presents together and jumped with joy, yelping with excitement as they opened each new gift. One of the older ones maturely exclaimed "Okay, this one's yours!" to her younger sibling, who burst into tears after struggling to claim someone else's gift as her own. The girls showed off their ballet moves and the boys demonstrated Tae Kwon Do kicks.

It was especially nice to spend time with my older daughter's in-laws. Her father-in-law, who is a physician as well as an accomplished pianist, always manages to create a concert hall with his piano performances whenever there is a family gathering (or, even, just a piano). He played Christmas carols, classical music, and the Korean national anthem. I was filled with gratitude as I sang along "Dong-hae-mul gwa Bak-doo-san yi mah-reu-go dal-do-rok . . ." I also saw happiness when I looked over at her mother-in-law, the Vice Mayor of the City of Alexandria, as she proclaimed "Wonderful!" and "I'm so proud!" as she doted on her daughter-in-law who gave birth to five grandchildren, in the order of daughter, son, daughter, son, daughter, all to their only son. It is hard to believe now that I always thought my daughter had to marry another Korean.

According to a study by a Stanford University medical school professor, William Frey, six-year-old kindergartners laugh about 300 times a day. However, during adulthood, that number diminishes by 95% to only 15 times a day. Laughter, a component to healthy bodies and minds, is a bonding agent for people. Why do people like people who laugh easily - It is because you get happier along with them - laughter is infectious. When you smile, a smile returns. When you look at a gloomy face, your face turns down in response. But when you look upon a brightly smiling face, your mood is lifted. There are people who give you joy just by being with you. When you are with someone who is confident and dignified, without arrogance, you become happy along with him or her. We should all live like children and laugh more! Every day, we should renew ourselves with optimism, affection, and generosity. It is essential in keeping healthy relationships that we remain friendly, but acknowledge privacy by keeping certain boundaries.

I remember an excerpt from a book I read, Fortune Comes to a Merry Home - "The best delight in life is that every day is new. The sun rises just like any other day but it isn't the same sun; a blossom blooms from the same tree but blooms differently each day." I would like to live more wisely by being more optimistic this year than the last, happily smiling, as the grand fortunes come through the door of a merry home.

Translation : Eunhwa Choe

수영 콘테스트

Swim Meet

전화벨이 울린다. 큰딸 목소리다.

"엄마, 바쁘게 지내다 보니 잊고 지날 뻔 했네요. 내일이 아버지날이에요."

아이가 다섯이다 보니 얼마나 정신이 없겠는가. 그래도 잊지 않고 뜻있는 날을 기억하고 챙겨주니 대견스럽기도 하고, 작은 딸네도 온다니 고맙기 그지없다.

리치몬드 큰 딸네에 도착해 초인종을 누르니 여섯 손주들이 와르르 현관으로 달려 나와 깡충깡충 뛰며 "할머니, 할아버지" 합창으로 반겨준다. 천사 같은 손주들이 있기에 딸네 집 나들이가 정말 행복하다. 작은 딸네 아이 셋, 합치면 여덟 손주. 이제 막 8개월된 손자(작은 딸), 손녀(큰 딸)

두 아기는 온 방을 기어 다니며 분주하기 그지없다.

베이비시터에게 여덟 손주들을 맡겨놓고 어른들만 외출이다.

미리 예약된 레스토랑에서 아버지날을 맞아 두딸과 사위들과 정겨운 대화속의 식사가 얼마나 마음 흐뭇하고 행복한 시간이었는지.

내일은 큰 손녀가 그 동안 배우고 익힌 수영 실력을 겨루는 콘테스트(Swim meet)가 있는 날이라니 기다려진다. 태양이 이글이글, 가만히 있어도 땀이 줄줄 흘러내리는 98도를 웃도는 무더운 날이다. 구름떼같이 몰려든 인파속에 수영장 가까이 담요(깔개)를 깔고, 음료수를 채운 아이스박스와 먹거리, 관람 준비하느라 부모들은 바삐 움직이며 법석이다. 시대의 흐름속에 정말로 아이들의 정서적인 과외활동에 적극적으로 참여하는 부모들의 열정이 보기 아름다웠다.

저녁 6시 정각. 정면에 자리한 무대 위에 오른 사회자의 대회선언에 이어 미국국가가 울려 퍼지고 수영 콘테스트가 질서정연하게 시작되었다. 연령별로 출전하는 선수(?) 들이 100여명. 5살~6살짜리 부터 마치 물위를 떠도는 아기 오리처럼 앙증맞다.

이제 7살~8살의 여섯 명의 선수들이 출전한단다.

7살인 손녀가 등장했다. 가슴은 쿵쿵 소리를 내고, 드디어 호루라기 소리에 맞추어 6명의 선수들이 물속으로 뛰어들어 재빨리 물살을 가르고, 응원부대들은 목이 터져라 아이들의 이름을 불러댄다. 할머니의 눈은 손녀에게 촛점을 정확히 맞추고 깜박임도 잊은 채 함께 헤엄쳐 나갔다.

드디어 우리 손녀가 일등으로 들어왔다. 수영장이 떠나가는 박수소리 그치지 않고. 용기와 끈기로 최선을 다한 7살의 어린 손녀의 모습이 얼마나 기특하고 장하든지. 정신없이 헤엄쳐 가는 중에도 자기 이름을 부르는 응원소리가 들렸다나.

밤 9시가 넘도록 이어진 수영 콘테스트. 피크닉을 겸한 가족애(愛)가 넘쳐나는 한바탕의 잔치라고 해야 꼭 어울릴 것 같다.

자라나는 아이들의 머리를 얼마나 쓰다듬었는가에 따라 어린 것의 바른 생활의 꽃이 피는 것. 그것은 정성의 손끝이요, 부모의 역할 또한 끊임없는 사랑과 관심, 더 나아가 모든 일에 적극적이고 긍정적인 자세를 보여주고 또 보여주어야 하는 것이 아닐까.

The phone rang. I heard my older daughter's voice on the line. "Mother, I've been so busy that I almost forgot that tomorrow is Father's Day." With five children, it must be quite a challenge for her to keep everything straight. Nonetheless, she hadn't forgotten this meaningful day. I was so proud of how she took care of all the arrangements, and especially thankful to learn my younger daughter's family would be coming, too.

We arrived at my older daughter's house in Richmond, Virginia. When we rang the doorbell, the response was a stampede of six grandchildren running and leaping toward the porch to greet us with a chorus of shouts, "Grandpa! Grandma!" My other two grandchildren, my older daughter's daughter and younger daughter's son, barely eight months old, were busy crawling all over the room inside. With such angelic grandchildren to see, each visit to my daughter's house is always a real treat. Adding to her five children my younger daughter's three, I am blessed to enjoy eight grandchildren.

We entrusted the children to a babysitter and headed out to eat, just the adults this time. I was so content and had such a wonderful time sharing a meal and warm conversation with my two daughters and their husbands in a restaurant they had reserved just for Father's Day. All the while, I was full of anticipation for my oldest granddaughter's swim meet the next day. It would be her chance to demonstrate the swimming skills she had been working so hard to master.

It was a very humid day. The sun was scorching hot. With temperatures reaching as high as 98 degrees, sweat was running down in beads even as we sat still. Ensconced in a sea of humanity that seemed to gather like clouds, we spread out a blanket to sit on and made preparations to watch the competition. Parents bustled about noisily preparing food and drinks they had stuffed into their coolers. It's so beautiful to see passionate parents so eager to support and participate in their children's extracurricular activities these days.

Promptly at 6:00 p.m., the moderator ascended onto the front stage and opened the event with a few remarks. This was followed by the playing of the national anthem, after which the meet was officially started. Everything was very well orchestrated.

There were about 100 athletes participating in the meet. It started with tiny tots aged 5 to 6 floating on the water like ducklings on a pond. After that it was the 7- and 8-year-olds' turn to compete. My 7-year-old granddaughter made her entrance. Their hearts pounding with excitement, the six swimmers dove into the water at the sound of the whistle. As they swiftly cut through the water, their land-based supporters screamed out their names repeatedly to cheer them on. My eyes were glued on my granddaughter; I didn't blink once as I vicariously swam the race with her.

Then it was over; she had finished in first place. Applause filled the facility and seemed to last forever. The courage and determination displayed by my 7-year-old granddaughter, who gave everything she had to win, was nothing less than admirable and truly praiseworthy. She said she could hear us calling out her name even while she was engrossed in her swimming. The swim meet continued until after 9:00 p.m. It was like a wonderful picnic and love-filled family celebration all combined into one wonderful event.

The degree to which our growing children mature to live proper lives is directly related to the number of times we stroke their hair with love. The true heart is felt through those finger tips. Is it not the role of every parent to not only show their children unending love and attention, but also to show them enthusiasm and positive support in everything they do?

Translation : Daniel Wessling

Kimchi and Rice

by Katie Pepper
(oldest grandchild, written when 7 years old)

A little girl named Emily loves kimchi and rice. It is a type of Korean food. Emily is Korean too. Her mother always cooks it for her. One cold foggy day Emily went to school. She liked everything about school except Caitlin.

Caitlin was the most popular girl at school and she made fun of Emily, because she is Korean. "What are you wearing?" laughed Caitlin. Emily frowned. She was wearing a hot pink Korean dress. At lunch, Emily sat next to her friend Samantha at the cafeteria table. "Did your mother pack you kimchi and rice again?" asked Samantha. Emily nodded. The cafeteria sounded like a giant playground.

When school was over, Emily sat on the bus with her other friend Caroline. "Nice dress," said Caroline. "Thanks," Emily answered with a Korean accent. At her bus stop, she stood up and ran to her house. By the time she got there, she immediately asked her mom for kimchi and rice. "How was school?" she asked. "Fine," she answered. She had never told her mom about Caitlin, because she didn't want to get her in trouble.

The next day, Caitlin asked, "Why do you have pencils in your hair?" Emily frowned again and walked away. She was sad at lunch, her locker and her classes and on the bus. When she got home she had to tell her mom about Caitlin. "Mom, there's this girl at school, Caitlin. Well she makes fun of me, because I'm Korean," said Emily. "I'm going to call her mom while you eat some kimchi and rice," said Emily's mom. Emily took her chopsticks and dug through the bowl and told herself always remember to tell an adult if someone is being mean.

The Big Wave

by Katie Pepper
(oldest grandchild, written when 7 years old)

One day I went to the beach with my family. It took about three hours to get there. When we finally got there, we unpacked our stuff. After that my mom and I went to the shore. My mom and I were, of course, wearing our bathing suits. When we got there, I saw seagulls, beach chairs, umbrellas, towels, sand castles, lifeguards and other people.

"Do you want to go boogie boarding?" asked my mom. "Sure," I answered. I had never gone boogie boarding before. "Here you go," my mom said as she gave me a boogie board. She also had one. I was a little scared, but when we went by the small waves it wasn't that bad. Then we saw a big wave. "Aahhhh!" I screamed as I turned my boogie board around and then the big wave hit our heads and took us into the sand. We both laughed and we did it again and again.

When we got back to the beach house I took a tiny nap with my Webkinz. After that I got up for dinner. "What's for dinner?" I asked. "Pizza," my Dad answered. I ate, then went to bed. We were at the beach for a week.

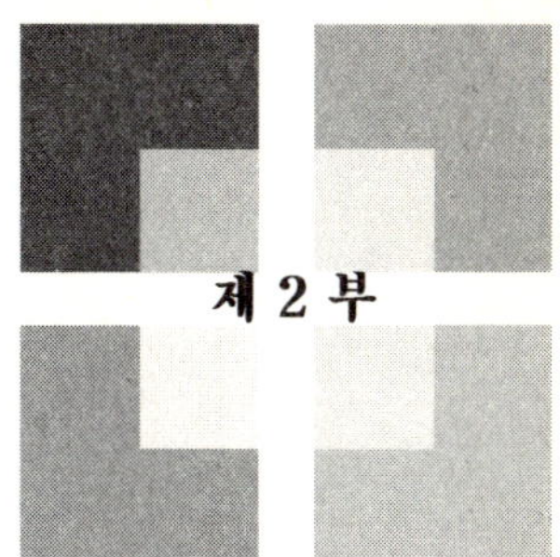

제 2 부

가을 단상

눈부시도록 하얗고 노란 들꽃들이 아직도 흐드러지게 피어있는 것을 보면 가을은 아직 깊지 않은듯 싶다. 그러나 하늘이 저렇게 구름 한 점 없이 드높고 푸른 걸 보니 가을 하늘은 완연하고, 윤기 잃어가는 나뭇잎들이 제 가끔 예쁜 색깔로 물드는 것을 보면 가을이 무르익어 가고 있음이 분명하다.

귀뚜라미도 또르르 또르르 맑은 음을 내며 풀섶에서 마구 울어대고, 아침은 아침대로, 낮은 낮대로 그 심상한 기온이 아주 적당하다. 밤은 더욱 그럴듯하다. 별 이라도 총총하면 재킷을 걸치고 나가 별 하나 나 하나 별을 세어가며 북두칠성도 찾아보는 멋진 가을밤을 노래하고도 싶어지고 잠들기가 아까워 책을 읽으며 미지의 것을 탐색하고 또 자신을 돌아보는데 가장 적절한 계절이기도 하다.

한여름 뜨거운 땡볕에 그을린 얼굴마다 가을 냄새가 흥건히 배어있는듯 신선함을 느낄 수 있어 더욱 좋다. 세월이야 원래 빠른 법이지만. 그래서 다들 화살처럼 빠르다고 푸념하는 바이지만 점점 짙어 가는 가을 풍경을 보면 폭염의 여름날이 먼 옛날로 여겨지기만 한다. 그렇게 덥고 끈질기던 땡볕은 이제 작별인 셈이다.

그러고 보면 계절도 한 생을 살고 있는지도 모른다. 봄 여름 가을 겨울의 사계보다 더 완벽한 생은 없다. 봄에 싹이 트고, 여름은 성장하여 가을엔 결실을 맺고, 겨울엔 휴식에 들어간다. 또 가을은 뭔가를 생각하게 하지만 욕망을 갖게도 하는 계절인 것 같다.

프랑스의 과학자이면서 철학자인 깨스롱 바헤라르(1884-1962)는 "참다운 삶을 살려고 하면 겸손하여야 한다. 자기의 삶을 너무 화려하게 포장하려고 하면 그는 더 이상 참다운 삶을 살 수가 없다"고 말했다. 그래서 인간은 겸손하고 성실하게 살아야 자기 성장과 충족을 가져올 수 있다고 생각한다.

나무는 그 종류에 따라 열매를 맺고 인간은 그 성격의 결과를 거둔다는 말이 있다. 인간은 모두가 한번 주어진 삶을 아름답고 행복하게 살 권리를 가지고 있기에 우리의 삶을 되돌아보며 더 나아가 진지하게 삶을 모색하며 끊임없이 사색하는 아름다움을 이 가을에 가져보는 것이 앞으로 더 나은 삶의 원동력이 되지않을까.

또한 가을은 누군가의 마음에 내 마음을 새겨 넣고 싶은 계절. 누군가에게 편지를 쓰고 싶은 계절이다. 사랑하는 사람에게는 내 사랑의 마음을, 미워하는 사람에게는 화해의 마음을, 나보다 가난한 사람에게는 따뜻한 축복의 마음을 전하고 싶어진다. 시간에 쫓기어 만나지 못하는 친척이나 친구가 어느 날 나의 편지를 받는다면 그들은 얼마나 즐거워할 것인가. 그립고 보고싶은 친척, 친구의 얼굴을 떠올리며 말하듯 글을 쓰는 낭만. 이 가을에 흠뻑 젖어보자.

그늘이 그리워지는 계절

뿌옇게 습한 공기를 자욱히 피워놓은 안개 낀 하이웨이를 조심스레 달려간다. 창 밖으로 스치는 검푸른 나무숲의 풍성함이 바라보는 마음까지 풍성해지는 이른 새벽, 골프장에서 친구들과 만나는 날이다.

보석처럼 반짝이는 작은 물방울을 매단 채 남들이 미처 밟지 않은 촉촉이 젖은 푸른 잔디밭을 여덟 개 발자국을 수없이 남기며 하늘 저편으로 조그마한 하얀 공을 날리며 힘차게 걷기 시작한다. 살랑이는 상큼한 바람과 물씬 풍기는 풀 내음, 탐스럽게 피어있는 노란 들꽃이 방긋 웃어주는, 행복을 여는 시간이다. 낮 기온이 90도를 넘는다는 일기예보에 맞춰 노출을 삼가며 나름대로 준비했지만 벌써부터 습한 더운 열을 뿜어대니 영락없는 사우나다.

오늘은 날씨 탓에 걷기를 포기하고 카트를 탓지만 , 평소에는 친구들과 골프백을 배낭처럼 등에 메고 어깨를 나란히 걸으며 나누는 다양한 대화 속에서 삶의 활력소를 얻곤 한다. 일부러 카트를 안 타는 이유는 많이 걸을 수 있는 효과 있는 운동을 하기 위함이며 걸을때마다 등에 진 골프백이 허리와 엉덩이 부분에 출렁거려주니 남의 손을 빌리지 않아도 절로 맛사지가 되어 기분 좋고, 골프백을 양어깨에 짊어질 때 양팔에 들어가는 힘이 양어깨와 팔관절에 많은 도움을 주며, 등산을 겸해 하는 좋은 운동이 되니 저절로 다이어트도 되고, 경제적이기도 하니, 일석이조가 아닌가. (꼭 필요한 골프채만 골라 아주 가볍게 만든 골프백을 선택해 넣음)

골프장에 자주 나타나 우리를 흥미로운 동물의 세계로 안내하는 선한 눈망울을 가진 사슴들도, 바위 틈사이에 굴을 파놓고 얼굴만 빼꼼 내밀고 눈치보는 여우새끼들의 귀여운 모습도, 멍청한 느림보 두더지들도, 발자국 소리에 지레 겁을 먹고 목을 움츠리는 거북이들도, 유난히 하얀 엉덩이를 뽐내듯 깡충거리는 들토끼들도, 새끼 사랑을 아끼지 않는 구스(오리 종류)들의 행렬까지도 오늘은 통 볼 수가 없다.

갑자기 더워진 날씨를 피해 나들이를 삼가며 그늘 밑에서 쉬고 있는 중일 테니 오늘은 참 아쉬운 날이다. 뜨겁게 내리쬐는 태양을 가릴 수 있는 나무 그늘이 있어 쉬어갈 수 있는 자연의 고마움과 덤으로 얻는 지혜와 낭만이 있어 삶이 즐거워지기도 한다.

이민의 고달픈 삶을 사는 우리들이지만 늘 겸손하고 성실하게 살면서 어렵고 외로워할 때 그늘이 되어주는 넉넉한 마음과 힘들고 고달팠을 때 그늘이 되어준 분들에게 진정으로 감사하는 마음으로 서로 섬기면서 사는 삶 속에서 서로서로가 자기 성장과 충족을 가질 수 있을 것이며, 삶의 형태는 같을 수 없지만 한번 주어진 삶이 더 아름답고 행복한 날들로 이어갈 수 있진 않을까.

그늘이 그리워지는 계절에 잠시 생각해본다.

꽃다운 시절의 추억을 불러준 영화들

'딩동' 초인종이 요란히 울린다.

급히 현관문을 여니 체격 좋은 우체부가 아담한 소포상자를 건네준다. 발송주소가 한국에서다. 누가 보낼을까? 황급히 열어보니 DVD 10개가 나온다. 내가 보고싶어 했던 한글 자막이 들어있는 영화들이다.

얼마전 큰딸과 Richmond다운타운에 있는 제퍼슨호텔에 간 적이 있었다.

이 호텔에서 Clark Gable과 Vivien Leigh가 주연한 그 유명한 영화 「바람과 함께 사라지다」의 몇 장면을 촬영했다고 하니 확인도 할 겸 옛 추억이 생각나 DVD를 빌려다 두 번이나 연거푸 보았는데 워락 영어가 짧아 속속들이 이해가 되지 않아 한글 자막이 있으면 얼마나 좋을까 말한 적이 있었는데 눈치 빠르게 큰딸이 인터넷을 통해서 한국으로 주문, 10편의 영화를 엄마 생일선물 깜짝 이벤트로 보내온 것이다.

영화 중 「로마의 휴일」 은 여고 1학년 때 학교 강당에 전교생이 모여 영화를 보면서 그 유명한 햅번스타일을 유행시킨 오드리 헵번의 청순한 아름다움과 매혹적인 핸섬가이 미남 그레고리 펙에 매혹되어 강당이 떠나가도록 환호성을 지르며 열광했던 10대 청소년시절이 되살아나기도 하고, 1929년의 헤밍웨이 원작을 바탕으로 부상당한 군인과 간호원의 애절한 러브스토리를 그린 「무기여 잘 있거라」 를 얼마나 보고 싶었으면 사복으로 갈아입고 들뜬 마음으로 영화보고 집에 왔을 때 학교를 빼먹은 것이 들통나 엄마에게 호되게 야단맞고 밤새 울어 짜리눈이 되었던 웃지 못할 추억을 안겨준 영화다.

공범이었던 내 친구는 지금 보스톤에서 잘 살고있다. 졸업 후 어느 날 친구 오빠가 졸업선물로 한 턱 쏘겠다고 (시세말로) 일찍 들어오라는 엄마의 허락하에 난생 처음 포크와 나이프를 써가며 근사한 저녁을 먹고 아카데미상 10개 부문을 휩쓴 명작 중의 명작 마가렛 미첼의 소설을 기초로 한 19세기 중반의 미국 남북전쟁을 배경으로 광활한 대지 위에서 펼쳐지는 웅대한 스케일의 영상과 숙명적인 로맨스를 그린 그 유명한 「바람과 함께 사라지다」 를 극장표가 매진되어 겨우 마지막 상영을 보고 늦게 돌아올 수밖에 없었는데 걱정이 되셔서 길목에서 기다리시던 엄마에게 밤늦게 다닌다고 꾸중을 듣고 엄마는 어쩜 저렇게 이해심이 없나 하고 못내 야속하여 이불 속에서 훌쩍거렸던 철없던 시절.

그 후로 친구 오빠와 데이트 하며 미래를 말하곤 했으나 세월의 바람과 함께 우린 서로의 길이 달라 그 오빠는 5남매를 둔 미개인(?)이 되어 성공한 사람 측에서 한국에서 살고 있고 난 산뜻하게 딸 둘만 낳은 현대인(?)으로 미국에서 어설픈 글쓰는 낭만에 젖어 감사하는 삶을 살고있다.

세월은 강물처럼 흘러 어느덧 산하에 단풍들고 낙엽지는 계절 가을이 온 것 같이 나도 이젠 가을 나이가 됐다. 철없던 시절에 느꼈던 야속함이 내가 자식 낳아 키우며 결혼 시키기까지 과정 과정에서 어머니의 한없는 사랑과 항상 겸손하고 성실하게 살라는 가르침을 떠올리며 가슴 저려하며 눈물지었는지 모른다.

한편 한편의 영화를 감상하며 생생하게 아스라이 멀어져간 먼 그 옛날 꽃다운 시절의 추억들이 새록새록 떠오른다. 지나간 추억들은 모두가 아름다운 것이려니.

만남의 즐거움

한겨울에도 소나무가 푸른 것은 올 봄에 낸 잎은 그대로 두고 작년 봄에 낸 잎들만 땅에 떨어뜨리기 때문이란다. 소나무 밑에 가지런히 쌓여있는 누렇게 뜬 소나무 잎들은 추워할 뿌리를 보호 하기라도 하는 양 세차게 부는 바람에도 안간힘을 쓰며 포근히 덮고 있다. 뒹구는 낙엽 따라 점점 추운 겨울로 치달으며 살짝 내린 첫 눈에 흥분할 때 오랜만에 미네소타에서, 뉴욕에서, 부부동반으로 먼 곳의 친구들이 나들이 왔다.

여고 졸업 40여년만에 이 곳 미국에서 만남을 시작으로 (우린 학창 시절엔 전혀 아는 척 하지 않은 사이였지만) 우린 긴장과 설렘으로 오가는 '정' 속에 익숙해지면서 우린 만나면 눈부시게 반갑고, 만나지 못하면 서로의 생각 속에 살다가, 오랜만의 만남 속에서도 전혀 거리감 없이 즐겁기만 하다.

남편들도 어느새 친구가 되어 골프를 즐기면서, 자랑하지 않으며 경쟁하지 않고 엄살 부려도 괜찮은 관계, 있는 그대로를 인정해주는, 세월따라 숙성해가는 포도주처럼 그렇게 무르익는 우정으로 노년의 무료함에 점점 활기를 불어 넣으리라. 요리를 잘 하는 친구를 주방장으로 갖가지 음식이 순식간에 만들어져 식탁에 오르고, 붉은 포도주로 건배를 들며 서로의 '건강을 위하여' 를 외치며 맛있는 저녁을 천천이 들며 담소 하기에 바빴다.

밤이 새도록 주고 받는 이야기 중에는, 지금 보다 더 나은 미래를 위한다는 명목아래 현재를 희생하고 있지는 않나? 과거에 사로잡혀 현재를 괴롭히지는 않나? 아무 생각도 없이 무의미하게 보내고 있지 않나? 를 주제로 잠은 저 멀리 달아나고 현재보다 소중한 시점이 없으니, 더 나이 들기 전, 이 겨울엔 따뜻한 곳으로 여행을 하자는 의견으로 뜻을 모으면서, 대접 받기보다 남을 먼저 생각하는 겸손한 사람들의 만남의 자리가 어울리는 밤이기도 했다.

잔잔한 클래식 음악이 흐르는 제과점에 들러 케익과 커피로 분위기를 잡고 네 커플이 한테 어울리는 만남의 즐거움은 한층 무르익어갔다.

마틴 루터가 "지구상에서 슬픔을 즐거움으로 만들고, 절망하는 사람에게 용기를 주며, 교만한 자를 겸손케 만들고 또 시기와 증오를 감소 시키는데 있어 음악처럼 딱맞는 치료법은 없다" 고 했듯이 좋아하는음악을 들으며 더 이상 늙지 않는 영혼과 마음을 고양시키는 아름다운 음률과 더불어 늘 푸르름을 보여주는 저 소나무같이 우리의 인생도 늘 푸르고 훨씬 푸근하게, 안정감있게, 멋지게 흘러가도록 무던히 노력해야 할 것이다.

배움의 기쁨

다시는 맞이할 수 없는 2005년은 저 멀리 가버리고 병술년 2006년의 새 아침이 밝은지 며칠이 지났다. 청명한 하늘에 뭉게구름이 서서히 피어 오르고 멀리 새소리가 정겹게 들려온다. 겨울 방학을 끝낸 아이들을 실어 나르는 노란 School Bus가 새벽부터 분주하게 움직이는 아침, 나는 오늘도 컴퓨터에 앉음으로써 하루를 시작하고 있다.

신형 컴퓨터를 구입한지 몇 달이 지났지만 촌스럽게도 난 그림의 떡이다. 남편은 열심히 두들기며 많은 정보를 찾으며 앤조이 하는데 난 언젠가는 배워야 겠다고 벼르기만 했지 과연 할 수 있을까? 자꾸 위축되기만 했다.

어느날 컴퓨터에 앉아 남편이 가르쳐주는 대로 '키 보드' 를 눌러본다.

제법 익숙해지기 시작, 정확도가 80%가 넘어가니 재미가 있어 몇 시간씩 컴퓨터에 앉아, 새로운 것을 배워 내 것이 될 때 느끼는 기분은 형용할 수 없는 기쁨의 충족감 그 자체다.

먼저 나의 딸들에게 이메일을 보내봤다. 나의 딸들은 엄마보다 더 신나하며 장하다고 추켜주기에 용기를 얻어 멀리 태평양 건너 고국의 친지, 친구들과 많은 시간을 요했던 편지도 이메일로 순식간에 오가며 정을 나누고 있다.

눈부시게 발전하는 정보시대에 사는 우린 현대문명 혜택에 감사가 절로 난다.

그야말로 컴맹에서 갓 벗어난 신출내기가 첫걸음을 배운 아기같이 철딱서니 없이 너무 홍분(?)하고 있는 건 아닐까. 이제는 신문사에 보내는 작품도 직접 이메일한다.

처음엔 한 시간 넘게 쓴 글이 다 날라갔을때 느끼는 억울함, 처참함, 기막힘이 가슴까지 '철렁' 소리가 나게하곤 했다. 다시 쓰려고 보면 지금껏 쓴 글이 전혀 생각나지 않아 가슴앓이하며 얼마나 끙끙댔는지 모른다.

더욱이 모교(여학교) 홈피에 들어가 창을 열면 선,후배님들, 또 동기동창들이 계시판에 올린 주옥같은 글과 갖가지 정보들, 또 주고받는 댓글에서 삶의 활력소가 넘쳐온다. 까맣게 잊혀질 뻔했던 우정을 홈피에서 찾으며 동기동창이란 40여 년이 지난 세월 속에서도 격의없이 서로 마음의 진실한 벗이 되어 숨김없이 마음문을 터놓고 의논도 하고 충고도 하면서 서로 잘되는 길을 일러줄 수 있기에 삶이 더 즐거워진다.

이렇게 우리의 삶은 끊임없는 만남 속에서 이어지는 신비의 체험이며 새로움을 창조하는 보람을 느낄 수 있는것이라 생각하며 열린 마음으로 모든 것을 순수하게 받아들이려는, 마음으로 배우며 생각하고 또 노력하려는 의지, 이것은 아직 내가 젊다는 것을 증명하는 것이 아닐까.

2006년 금년에도 더 많은 배움의 기쁨을 갖고 싶다.

봄의 향기와 그리움의 파도

춥고 칙칙했던 긴 겨울을 밀어내고 소리없이 봄은 왔다.

봄은 정녕 기쁨에 싸인 계절이며 생명이 약동하는 계절이다. 흠뻑 물오른 수양버들은 가지마다 온통 연두빛을 휘감은채 불어오는 봄바람에 살랑살랑 춤을추며, 꽃샘추위속에서도 본격적인 봄기운을 뿜어대는 대 자연의 법칙을 누가 막을 수 있겠는가. 자연은 어김없이 빨, 주, 노, 초, 파, 남. 보의 예쁜 색깔과 눈부시도록 하얀 꽃들을 피워내며 봄 향기에 마냥 젖는 즐거움을 주고있다.

봄을 맞아 한층 경쾌해진 새들의 합창소리가 멋 스럽게 들려오고, 아이들의 재잘거리는 소리에 딸네 집에서 첫 아침을 맞이한다. 네 아이들의 분주한 움직임에 온통 마음을 빼앗기며, 어느새 서툰 걷기운동에 뒤뚱거리는 돌 잡이 손자는 당연 1위의 인기를 끌며 웃음꽃을 피어준다. 여섯살,

네살, 두살의 형, 누나들의 극성스러움에도 귀찮게 동생이 귀엽다고 볼에 뽀뽀하며 한데 엉켜 뒹굴고 서로 좋아라 깔깔대는 모습들, 싸우다가도 한 쪽이 울면 자기것이라 우기던 장난감도 선뜻 내주는 양보심, 달랑 외동일 때 보다는 어울려 노는 모습에서 다정함을 본다.

형제많은 아이들이 정서면에 뛰어난다니, 그래서 나의 딸들은 저마다 아이 많이 낳기에 열을 올리나보다.

문뜩, 그 옛날 나의 어린시절, 부모님의 한없는 사랑을 받으며, 나의 6형제가 한데 어울려 낄낄거리며 뛰놀던 그 시절이 그리워짐을 숨길 수 없으며, 애틋한 수많은 추억 속에 한참을 빠져서 서성거려본다. 이제는 모두 가족을 이루고 제 가끔 삶에 충실하다. 열심히 살아간다는 것은 행복을 말하는 것이고 기쁨을 만드는 일이다. 무엇보다도 모두가 건강함속에서, 부지런히 살아가는 즐거움처럼 여유있는 인생은 없다고 생각하며 감사한다.

가족이 지니는 의미는 그냥 단순한 사랑이 아니라 지켜봐 주는 누군가가 거기 있다는 것, 바로 정신적인 안정감을 느껴가며 행복을 갖게 되는것이 아닐까. 가족말고는 그 무엇도 그걸 줄 순 없다고 생각한다.

더 나아가 자라나는 어린 아이들에게는 끈임없는 사랑과 관심속에서, 그리고 모든 일에 적극적이고 긍정적인 자세를 보인다면 어른들이 모르는 사이에 성숙하고 슬기롭고 강인하게 자랄 것이라 생각해본다.

긴 겨울을 벗어나 봄이 온 것 같이 내 몸 안의 어디엔가 숨어있을 싱그러운 기운 같은것이 몸 안 가득 고이도록 애써야 할 것이다. 이제 시간의 흐름에 따라 점점 세월도, 기쁨도, 슬픔도 구름처럼 지나가리라. 그러나 나는 인생의 무상함을 아는 나이가 된다고 해도, 내 인생의 봄을 향하여 힘차게 나아가리라. 모든 생명이 빛과 따사로움을 향하여 나아가듯이.

그리고 봄의 향기와 함께 내가 살아온 시간 속에 추억들이 그리움의 파도가 되어 출렁출렁 정겹게 밀려오고 또 밀려 올 것이다.

비우며 사는 나이

뒤뜰에 서 있는 나무들은 뜨거운 한 여름이 돼서야 한창 푸르름이 무르익으며 녹색 병풍을 펴 놓은 듯 아늑한 별장의 분위기를 만들어준다. 온몸을 빨간 색으로 치장한 예쁜 새가 우리 뒤뜰로 나들이 왔다. 자연에 순응하며 과욕을 내지 않고 소박한 삶을 즐기는 저 새들을 닮아 저 푸른 창공을 한없이 나는 상상의 나래를 펴보며. Deck에 나가 앉아 문듯 지나쳐간 시간들을 떠올리며 회상해 본다.

누구나 다 구름 같고 무지개 같은 환상 속에서 한때를 보낸 기억을 지니고 나이를 더해간다. 몇 년 전만해도 새벽 6시에 일어나 서둘러 화장하고 출근시간 맞추느라 막혀있는 차선을 요리조리 바꾸며 동동거리며 달리던 그 시간들, 하품이 나올정도로 퇴근시간을 알리는 시계추를 바라보며, 다람쥐 쳇바퀴 돌 듯 같은 일을 반복하며 지겨워했던 일들, 우체국 직원이 되어 저녁일을 했기에 식구들과 오붓한 저녁식사를 함께 할 수 없음을 나의 두 딸들이 무던히도 투정했던 안쓰러운 추억들이 저 멀리 가고 있다.

비즈네스 하면 잘 할텐데 주위에서 마냥 부추겼지만 고집했던 직장생활, 유년 시절 아버지께서 사업하시며 많은 어려움을 겪으시고, 남에게 사기도 당하시고 자금난으로 어머니께서도 엄청나게 마음고생 하시는 것을 보며 성장하면서 난 절대 비즈네스는 안 할것이며 결혼도 샐러리맨으로 거기 틀에 맞추어야지 하는 것이 내 생활신조였다.

점점 안정된 중류생활로 접어들었지만 6·25를 겪으며 또 가난한 시절이 있었기에 나 자신이나 가족들의 지나친 낭비나 경제적 허영 같은 것에는 크게 맘쓰지 않고 살았다. 가난을 선하게 체험한 사람은 어떻게 사는것이 값있는 것인가를 뒤늦게 깨닫게 된다고 생각하기도 하면서.

딸들이 대학을 졸업하고 좋은 직장을 갖게되고 네 식구가 단란함 속에서 지내던 어느 날 큰딸이 사귀던 미국 백인청년을 데리고 왔다.

미국에서 30년 넘게 살았는데도 고루한 답답함이 큰딸 마음을 서운하게 했었다. 큰딸이 결혼하고 그 다음 해에는 작은딸도 결혼해 집을 떠나니 둘만 남게된 텅 빈 집안에 강아지 뽀삐가 유일한 귀여움을 안겨주었다. 이제는 두 딸들이 열심히 세 손자, 세 손녀의 할머니로 만들어주어 바쁜 나날 속에서 아이들의 재롱에 흠뻑 파묻혀 때론 힘들기도 하지만 즐거움 속에서 생기는 잔주름이 억울하거나 싫지만도 않은 당연한 삶의 훈장이라고 미소짓기도 한다.

한때 큰딸 마음을 서운케 했던 이민 1세인 엄마의 마음을 큰딸이 이해해주니 고맙고, 나 또한 자기 아내와 자식들과 가정밖에 모르는 충실한 사위들이 이쁘고 대견스럽기 그지없으니 감사할 뿐이다. 큰 집에서 자그마한 집으로 옮기고 살림을 정리하느라고 했으나 아직도 차고엔 아까워서 버리지 못한 것이 꽉 차있다. 이러다가 누가 먼저라도 떠나가면 남은 사람 추억을 껴안은 채 슬퍼 하는 수고를 덜기 위해서라도 정리 해야한다.

이 세상에서 가장 큰 부자는 가진 것에 만족할 줄 아는 사람이라고 한다. 있는 것에 만족하며 남편과 같은 취미로 푸른 잔디를 밟으며 은퇴생활을 즐길 수 있는 축복을 주신 하나님의 무한한 사랑에 감사 하며, 비우며 사는 황혼의 나이를 맞아 첫 단추를 건강하고 긍정적인 자세로 잘 끼워가며 아름다운 삶을 가꾸며 살아 가리라.

슬픈 이별

체감온도 100도를 훨씬 넘는 무더운 날이다. 갑자기 쏟아 붓는 소나기가 뜨겁게 달군 대지를 식히느라 아스팔트의 열기가 확확 숨을 몰아쉬며 뿌연 김을 마구 뿜어댄다. 하늘을 가를듯 번득이는 불빛과 우당탕 질러대는 자연의 소리가 계속되는 오후 한때. 20년이 훨씬 넘은 그날도 이렇게 소나기가 마구 퍼부었다.

뉴욕에 살고있는 친구의 비보를 듣고 기막혀 분노했던 그날의 추억이 자꾸 슬픈 연민의 늪으로 빠져들게 한다. 10년의 열렬한 연애 끝에 결혼하고 첫아들을 낳아 첫돌 며칠을 앞둔 어느 날, 모두가 부러워하는 좋은 직장의 엘리트로 잘나가던 신랑이 불행하게도 교통사고로 세상을 떠났다. 갑자기 당한 슬픔을 어떻게 이겨야 하나 울부짖던 친구는 아기와 살아야 겠다는 일념으로 남편이 남겨놓은 자금으로 정신없이 뛰었다. 어느 정도

자리가 잡히기 시작할 즈음 자신의 존재와 의미에 대해서 종종 회의가 생겼고, 앞으로의 생활 진로에 대한 갈등 속에서 미래를 위해 투자하기로 굳게 마음먹고 미국행을 결심했단다.

서양속담에 "하늘이 비를 내리기로 결정하고 어머니가 재혼하기로 마음먹으면 막을 도리가 없다" 했는데 주위에서 그렇게 말렸는데도 친구는 어린아들을 친정에 맡기고 캐나다를 경유, 어렵사리 미국에 왔다. 처해있는 현실이 힘들고 버거워도 영주권 받고 다시 만난다는 희망으로 이를 견뎠다. 그날도 영주권 수속을 위해 변호사를 만나고 나오는 길에 어처구니없는 교통사고를 당했다.

사고차는 보험에 가입하지 않은 뺑소니 차였다. 연고자 없이 노동허가서만 받은 신분으로 시립병원에 입원해있다는 소식을 뒤늦게 듣고 허겁지겁 찾아간 나는 독방에 누워있는 친구의 모습을 보고 기겁을 했다.

눈은 초점을 잃고 목과 양팔에 연결된 흰 붕대로 매어져 양팔이 좌우로 허공을 향해 기계처럼 허우적거리는 몰골로 변한 괴물(?) 이 되어 있었다. "너, 이 꼴로 병원에 누워 있으려고 미국 온 거 아니잖아. 말 좀 해봐, 이 바보야." 소리치며 떼를 썼지만 아무 대답이 없다. 그래도 내가 누군지는 알았나보다. 심장박동 모니터에 그려지는 파장이 갑자기 널뛰기를 한다. 급히 수속해 온 아들과 한마디 대화도 나누지 못한 채 어처구니없는 삶의 종말을 맞고 말았다.

시련과 아픈 경험을 통해 세상을 관망할 줄 아는 통찰력을 가졌고 무한한 가능성을 가진 친구였는데, 얼마나 가엾고 불쌍한지 난 뉴욕으로 정신없이 달렸다. 후러싱의 한 장의사에서 목사님을 모시고 쓸쓸하게 치러진 장례식. "내 영혼이 은총 입어 중한 죄짐 벗고보니 슬픔 많은 이세상도 천국으로 화하도다." 찬송을 부르며 얼마나 울었는지. 유일한 자기의 분신인 아들을 홀로 남겨두고 이 세상을 떠나는 엄마의 기막힌 운명, 화장터에서

한 줌 재로 변한 상자를 품에 안고 오열하는 아들, 엄마없는 고국으로 돌아가야 하는 아들의 처지, 이보다 더한 슬픈이별이 또 있을까. 이 친구가 생각나는 날이면 지금도 메어지는 가슴을 달래느라 한참을 애써야 한다.

정말로 행복한 사람

오랜 동안 가뭄이 계속되어 얼마나 애타게 비를 기다렸던가. 주말 내내 아스팔트를 난타하듯 퍼부어 대던 비가 목말랐던 대지 위를 흠뻑 적시며 갈증을 시원스럽게 해소시켜 주었다.

흩날리는 낙엽 속에 점점 깊어 가는 가을, 나무잎들은 분첩을 꺼내 든 것처럼 붉은 기운을 진하게 덧칠하고 있고, 떨어지는 가을잎을 보면 아직도 마음 한구석에 계절이 주는 사색의 향기를 느낄 수 있다. 가을 중턱에서 울어주는 귀뚜라미 소리에 잠 못이루며 이리저리 뒤척거리는 것은 아직 마음에 젊은 감성이 그대로 살아있다는 것을 말해주는 것일 테니 건강하게 움직이며 살아있음을 실감할 수 있으니 얼마나 큰 축복인가. 살아있으므로 가능성의 의미를 가질 수 있는 것이고 죽은 자에게는 기대할것이 전혀 없는 것이다. 그래서 사람과 사람 사이에 가장 필요한 것은 서로 의

지하며 삶을 유익하게 살 수 있도록 상부상조하며 사는 삶이다.

그렇다면 어떻게 살아야 하나, 인간이 인간을 아는길은 독서를 통해서이다. 다른 사람의 삶이 어떠한 것인가를 알기 위해서라도 틈틈이 책을 읽으며 내 삶의 폭을 넓혀 보다 나은 내일의 삶을 개척하며 꿈꾸어야 한다. 꿈꾸는 사람은 행복한 사람이라고 한다. 꿈은 인간의 삶을 현실의 세계에서 환상의 세계로 옮겨놓기도 하고, 꿈은 인간을 보다 나은 세계로 끌고가는 힘을지니게 한다.

밝게 개인 오늘 아침 햇살이 눈부시게 창으로 들어와 식탁에 놓인 흑장미 꽃병 위에 환하게 쏟아내고 있다. 나는 이 아침도 나이에 걸맞게 예나 다름없이 노래와 웃음 라인댄스 같은 소박한 즐거움에 도취되는 시간을 많이 갖곤 한다. 또한 이 아침에 누가, 아니 나의 딸들이 사람이 사는일, 사는 삶이 무엇이냐고 묻는다면 나는 자라기 위해서 살고 열매맺기 위해서 산다고 말해주고 싶다. 하지만 열매란 그냥 열리는 것이 아니라 수많은 고통 속에서도 피나는 노력과 인내로 말미암아 단물이 고여 맺어지는것이기에 자기 몫의 삶을 잘 챙겨야 할 것이다 라고 일깨워 주고도 싶다. 그러나 너무 빡빡하게 사는 삶 보다 좀 느긋하게 차 한잔이라도 마시면서 뭔가 대화도 나누고 조금은 여유를 가지며 사는 삶, 그것이 우리의 삶의 질을 높이는 것이라고 대답해주고 싶다.

어느 정신과 의사가 말하기를 불행하게도 정신질환자는 대개 부유한 가정 출신이 많다고 한다. 부가 결코 행복이나 만족감 까지 가져다주지 못하는 것 같다. 돈이 다정함을 대신 할 수 없고 권력도 다정함을 대신 할 수 없다는 뜻이다. 가진 것에 만족하고 사는 삶이 행복을 부르는 삶이 아닐까.

행복은 진정 마음의 거울에 비쳐진 자아의 모습에서 찾을 수 있는 것이지 결코 누가 어떻게 마련해 줄 수 있는 것은 아니다. 그러기에 더욱 어떠한 세속적 고통이나 어려움 속에서도 삶이 가치 있는 것이라 믿는 이야말로 정말로 행복한 사람일 것이다.

추억이 함께 가는 연기자

파란 하늘에 아무 거리낌 없이 떠있는 흰구름 송이를 바라보며 넓게 펼쳐진 잔디를 밟고 걷는 순간이다. 자꾸 두리번거리며 찾던 여우가 바로 눈앞에 어슬렁거리며 나타난 것이다. 반가웠다.

작년 봄이었다. 골프장 한 언덕 비스듬한 바위틈 작은 동굴 밖으로 빠끔히 얼굴을 내민 여우새끼들의 까만 눈동자들이 우리들의 발자국 소리에 놀라 움칠하며 몸을 숨긴다. 그곳을 지날 때마다 귀여운 아기 여우들을 찾곤 했지만 어디로 갔는지 통 보이지 않더니 어느날 깡마른 몸집에 온통 흙칠을 하고 한 마리가 나타났다.

배고픔이 역력한 여우는 발까지 절고 있는 폼이 너무 불쌍해 보인다.

이날은 흠뻑 허기에서 벗어나 행복한 몸짓으로 숲속으로 사라지는 모습을 보면서 배고픔의 서러움을 잠시 생각해 본다.

배고픔이 어디 동물의 세계 뿐이겠는가.

나도 피난시절 배고픔을 경험했고 저 북한 어린이들, 아프리카 등지의 어린아이들의 깡마른 모습이 눈에 아른거린다. 언제나 배고픔이 없는 풍족한 세상이 될는지.

세상보다 자연생태계에서 더 많은 것을 배운다. 나무는 바람이 불거나 눈이 오거나 시비를 걸지않는다. 자기있는 모습 그대로 서 있다. 왜 그럴까, 뿌리가 깊기 때문일 것이다. 오직 순리대로 마음 편히 건강하게 사는 것이 가장 큰 행복의 비결임을 잊지 말아야 할 것이며 사는 것은 끈임없는 자연의 순환과 같은것이다.

이민 초기에는 참으로 힘들고, 고달파서 울었고 또 외로워서도 울었다. 한두 번 쯤은 자기를 돌아보면서 후회와 원망 그리고 자기의 어리석음에 대한 자기성찰의 기회를 가져보기도 하면서 서로 의지하며 삶을 유익하게 살 수 있는 상부상조하는 삶, 보기에도 얼마나 아름다운지.

교황 바오로 2세가 임종할 즈음 마지막 한 말은 "나는 행복합니다. 여러분들도 행복하십시오." 였다고 한다. 인생의 마지막 순간에도 슬픔과 고독 그리고 후회가 가슴에 응어리지지 않고 행복했다고 고백하는 것은 한 순간에 일어난 감정이 아닐 것이다. 그렇게 살아왔고 또 그렇게 살기를 바라는 신앙인의 긍정적인 태도의 결과일 것이다.

하늘에는 황혼이 물어온다. 구름발 사이로 번져오고 있는 붉은 황혼은 서서이 어둠으로 변해간다. 인생이 백년도 버티기 어려운데 천만년 살 것 같이 타협할 줄 모르는 것이 우리 인생들이다. 우리의 삶은 순간순간마다 끝없는 선택을 해야 한다. 선택이라는 것은 전적으로 본인 스스로 하는 것이 아니겠는가 . 순간의 선택들이 하나하나 모여 우리 인생의 모습을 아름답게 만들어가면서, 세월의 힘은 속이지 못해 얼굴엔 주름이 보이지만 나는 미련의 끈을 잡지않고 명쾌한 웃음을 갖으려고 무던히 애쓰며 노력하려고 한다.

우리가 언제까지 젊게만 있을 수 없는 것이 아닌가. 이젠 시간의 흐름에 몸을 맡기며 추억이 함께 가는 연기자로 남고 싶다

친구 이야기

뉴욕 사는 여고 동창생에게서 전화가 왔다. 미국 전역에 사는 동기생들이 더 늙기 전에 부부동반으로 멋지고 아름다운 여행을 하자는 내용이다. 꼭 부부동반이어야 한다는 조건이다. 그렇지 않아도 터키, 그리스는 꼭 한 번 가보고 싶은 곳이어서 간다고 했지만 남편은 단체 여행을 그리 달가워하지 않아 분명 여자들끼리 가라고 할 터이다.

친구는 10여 년 전에 15박 16일로 다녀온 기막힌 추억이 있다며 유럽여행담을 털어놓는다. 영국 히드로 공항에서 각처에서 온 40여 명과 가이드와 만나 한 팀이 되어 버스로 여행을 시작, 브뤼셀, 네델란드 등을 거쳐 극치의 자연미를 자랑하는 스위스에 도착하기까지 여행은 너무 즐거웠다.

점심을 먹으러 식당에 들어갔다. 빨리 움직여야 단체행동에 보조를 맞출 수 있는데 남편이 어찌나 늑장을 부리는지 빨리 오라고 신호를 보냈단다. 그러나 남편은 느릿한 걸음으로 식탁에 와 앉더니 느닷없이 자기 발등을 사정없이 밟았다. 일행이 눈치챌까봐 비명도 못 지르고, 얼굴은 웃고 눈물이 찔끔 나오는 것을 참았다. "조용하고 착한 남편이 별안간 폭군이 되다니 간 큰 남자가 따로 있는게 아니구나" 생각하며 이럴 땐 어떻게 하나 안절부절 한참을 화를 속으로 삼키며 궁리하다 일단은 모른 체 하기로 했다고 했다.

알프스 설경에 매료되고, 빙하가 할퀴고 간 면도날처럼 뾰족한 고봉들 사이로 바닥까지 훤히 보일 것 같은 알파인 호수의 그림 같은 풍경에 감탄하며 호텔에 돌아와 보니 발등에 멍이 시퍼렇게 들어 있었다. 슬펐다. 그러나 남편은 발등 밟은 기억은 전혀 없어 보이고 이왕 비싼 경비 들여 온 여행인데 이 문제가 거론되면 피차 남은 여행이 엉망이 될 것 같아 침묵으로 인내하며 혼자 가슴앓이를 했다.

마지막 여행지 프랑스 관광을 끝내고 공항 대합실에서 미국행 비행기를 기다리면서 슬며시 멍든 발등을 보여 주었단다. 남편은 깜짝 놀라며 어떻게 된 거냐고 묻는데, 정말 몰랐던 것인지, 자초지종 설명을 듣고 나서는 생각이 난다며 "어련히 가서 앉을 텐데 일행도 많은데 아이같이 보채는 것 같아 순간 화가 났었다" 고 말했단다. 그리고는 "혼자 가슴앓이 하면서도 좋은 여행을 위해 내색 안하고 참아줘서 고맙고 사랑스럽다" 고 하면서 신사도를 벗어난 비겁한 행동이 부끄럽다고 용서를 구했단다.

갑자기 지혜로운 친구의 얼굴이 보고 싶어진다. 서양 속담에 "결혼 후 3개월은 서로 관찰하고, 3년은 사랑하고, 그리고 30년은 용서하며 살아간다"는 말이 있다. 모르는 사람끼리 만나 한 지붕 밑에서 평생을 같이 산다는 것은 그 자체가 예술행위에 준하는 고도의 창작세계라고 생각한다.

후두둑 소리를 내며 소나기가 지붕을 한없이 두드리는 밤이다. 친구야, 세상 다하는 날까지 참으며 용서하며 사랑하며 멋진 삶을 살기 바란다.

행복은 충족감의 꽃이다

봄날 같던 날씨가 오늘은 기온이 뚝 떨어져 몹시 춥다.

차가운 세찬 바람에 나무 가지들이 몸부림치며 어쩔 줄 몰라 한다

따사로운 햇볕이 너무 좋아 나는 창가에 앉아 뜨거운 유자차를 마시며 지난날의 추억 속으로 가본다.

세월은 물처럼 흘러간다. 지난해 가을이 무르익은 10월 중순 우리 부부는 서울 한복판에 우뚝선 남산을 오르고 있었다. 남산을 오르내리는 케이블카가 있는데도 든든한 발로 뛰다시피 오르다가 힘들면 잠깐 쉬고 하면서 정상에 올랐다.

남산 꼭대기에 자리한 팔각정에 모여 앉은 많은 등산객들. 주위는 예전의 모습을 다 잃어버리고 서울 타워가 하늘을 찌를 듯 서 있다. 티켓을 사서 237m의 높이를 자랑하는 서울 타워 전망대에 오르고 또 더 한층 올라

가 360도 회전전망대 레스토랑에 들어가 앉아 커피를 주문하고 서울 시가지를 내려다보는 전경은 너무 아름다웠다. 저 멀리 북한산성이 보이고 청와대가 보이고.

어린시절 오빠와 등교길인 남산길을 오가며 벚나무에 올라가 버찌를 따 마구 떨어뜨리면 난 오빠의 모자를 거꾸로 쥐고 주워 담으며 깔깔대며 달고 맛있는 버찌를 씹을 때 톡톡 터져 검정물에 온통 얼굴이며 손과 옷에 범벅이 됐던 그 시절이 그리워진다. 핑크색 예쁜 치마저고리를 받쳐입고 검정 양복을 흰 와이셔츠에 빼 입은 막 약혼식을 끝낸 신랑신부가 무지개 꿈을 안고 수줍게 웃으며 남산을 오르며 데이트하던 그 추억이며, 아기 아빠 엄마가 되어 아기와 함께 처음 장만한 검정 세단 자가용을 타고 팔각정에 올라(그때는 차가 올라갔다)시내 야경을 내려다보며 미지의 미국 행을 꿈꾸던 1970년의 그 시절이 뭉게뭉게 구름이 피어나듯 추억 속에 빠져든다. 30여 년이 지난 지금 먼 옛 일들을 떠올리면 그것은 언제나 하나의 꽃으로 피어오른다. 살아온 날들을 뒤돌아보는 이력의 세계는 언제나 잡다한 아름다움 뿐이다.

서울의 밤은 가로등들이 다 차지하고 있다 , 환한 대낮처럼 불을 밝히고 울긋불긋 간판들과 전광판을 스치며 분주히 차량이 붐빈다. 먼동이 틀 때 서울을 벗어나 용평으로 가는 차창밖에는 가을의 온갖 단풍이 황홀하게 타고 있고 휴게소에 쉬면서 뜨거운 우동을 사먹으며 가까이 간 강원도 속초 근처엔 짭쪼롬한 바다의 비릿한 냄새가 물씬 풍겨온다. 설악산 오색 약수터엔 가뭄으로 갈증을 해소할 수 없어 안타까움을 남기고 한계령을 넘으며 펼쳐져 있는 카펫 모양 포근하게 깔려있는 단풍 물결이 어우러져 우뚝우뚝 뾰족뾰족 솟은 바위산 대자연의 절경 앞에 감탄하며 자연은 정직하고 언제나 인간 앞에 진실하게 살기를 보여주는 것 같아 즐거움 속에서도 엄숙해지기도 했다. 그러나 지금껏 살면서 언제나 한번쯤, 아니 몇 번씩 절룩거리며 살고 이 절룩거림이 있기에 인간다울 수 있는 것이라고 생각하며 오늘의 나를 본다. 고국의 가을하늘은 유난히 높고 파랗다.

그 동안 고국 나들이 때면 짧은 직장 휴가를 이용해 수박 겉핥기 식으로 형제 친척 친구들을 그저 인사치레로 만나곤 했다. 이제는 느긋한 시간의 여유를 가지며 넉넉한 만남의 소중함 속에서 기쁨을 누리며 미처 깨닫지 못했던, 발이 닿지 않은 곳도 찾으며 고국에서의 행복을 마냥 느낄 수 있었다.

행복, 그것은 생각의 방법에 따라 이루어지는 충족감의 꽃이라고 말하고 싶어진다.

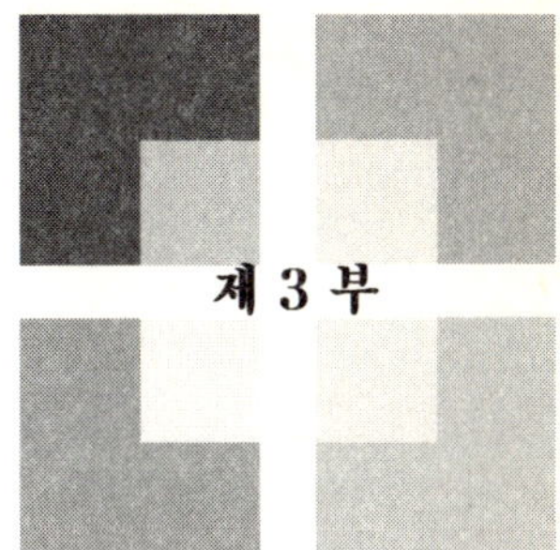

제 3 부

43년만의 만남

근 1년 전 죽은 듯 누렇게 뜬 나뭇가지마다 파릇파릇 새싹이 돋아나고 노오란 개나리꽃, 벚꽃이 꽃망울을 터뜨리기 시작하며 물이 잔뜩 올라 온통 연두빛으로 휘감은 축 늘어진 수양버들 가지들이 살랑살랑 부는 봄바람에 맞추어 춤추던 작년 이맘때다.

42년. 긴 세월동안 까맣게 잊고 살았던 여고졸업반 시절 내 짝꿍이던 친구로부터 느닷없이 전화가 걸려왔다. 얼마나 놀라고 반가웠는지 이게 얼마 만인가.

친구는 얼굴도 예쁘고 늘 일등을 도맡아 하는 반장으로 그와 짝으로 공부에 열을 올렸던 학창시절의 추억으로 마냥 빠져 들어간다.

그 후 우린 편지로 전화로 그 긴 세월의 궁금증을 풀기에 무척이나 바쁜 나날을 보냈다. 친구는 결혼해서 세아이의 엄마가 되고도 교편생활을 하면서 젊은 시절을 보냈고 나는 결혼해 미국에 와 이민생활 하느라 젊은 시절을 정신없이 보냈다.

친구는 한국에서 나는 미국에서 10년이면 강산이 변한다는데 강산이 4번 변하고도 3년이나 지났으니 얼마나 많이 변했을까 정말 보고싶어진다.

그런데 그 친구가 미국에 온단다. 첫 방문지는 미네소타. 미네소타에 사는 동창 친구가 한국에서 오는 친구와 합류하자며 자기 집으로 초대하는 비행기표를 보내왔다. 흰 구름이 잔잔히 깔린 하늘 저 끝에 길게 걸려있는 주황색으로 붉게 물든 석양이 하루를 마감하며 활활 타오르다 어두움이 서서히 깔리면서 빛을 잃어가고 있다.

친구 부부의 마중을 받으며 공항을 벗어난다. 길가에 쌓여 있는 눈이 높은 산을 만들었고 눈 덮인 지붕은 내려앉을 정도다. 내일, 내일이면 짝꿍을 만난다. 밤새 방방 뛰는 여고시절 소녀의 기분에 사로잡혀 잠도 설친 채 서둘러 공항으로 달렸다. 햇빛이 쨍쨍한데도 눈은 계속 내리고 있다.

기다리는 시간이 어찌나 긴지 조바심 치는데 카트를 밀고 나오는 한 중년여인. 낯설기는 했지만 역시나 내 친구가 맞다. 반가움에 한동안 포옹하고 놓지 못했다. 단발머리에 풀먹여 눈부시도록 하얀 칼라 빳빳하게 다려 단정하게 입던 우리의 꿈많고 도도했던 시절과 43년이란 긴 세월은 어디로 눈 깜짝할 사이에 지나가고 머리에 서리가 내린 이 나이에 우리는 만났다.

얌전하던 친구는 많이도 변해 얼마나 익살스러운지 한마디 던질 때마다 웃음보가 터진다. 여고시절 서슴지 않고 썼던 우리들만의 허락된 대화가 누가 먼저랄 것도 없이 자연스럽게 흘러 나왔다. 지칠 줄 모르고 떠들어대는 세 여인의 목소리가 얼마나 씨끄러울까.

버지니아로 돌아왔다가 뉴욕,미시간으로 향한 자동차 여행, 미시간 친구 부부와 다 함께 예정에 없던 나이아가라 관광을 떠났다. 여권, 시민권증도 없이 운전면허증 하나로 국경을 넘나드는 배짱을 부렸다.

추운 겨울 2월에 가본 나이아가라폭포는 변함없이 우렁찬소리를 질러대며 쏟아 붓고 있었지만 폭포 주위는 온통 잉크를 뿌려 번진 듯한 크고 우람한 얼음 조각들로 뒤덮여 장관을 이루고 근처 나무들도 쉬지 않고 뿜어대는 물방울을 피할 수 없어 가지마다 수정 같은 고드름을 매달았고 여기저기에 예쁘게 피어오른 쌍무지개를 펼쳐 놓았다.

가는 곳마다 동기생들이 살고 있어 화끈한 환영을 받으며 감격의 시간들이 아쉽게 지나갔다. 우리의 뒤늦은 43년만의 만남이 영원토록 변치 않는 멋진 우정으로 이어갈 것이다.

가을의 노래

언제 부턴가 가을 빛이 막 나무잎에 찾아오르기 시작할 무렵, 분첩을 꺼내든것 처럼 나무 잎들은 고운 빛깔로 덧칠하더니 이제는 황홀한 울긋불긋 아름다운 환상의 단풍으로 물들여 놓은 가을의 중심을 넘고 있다.

세월은 강물 처럼 흐른다. 어느새 산하에 낙엽의 계절이 성큼 다가서고 있으니 말이다. 가을은 성장과 번성을 지나 거둠과 결실의 계절이기도 하지만, 퇴락하는 서글픔도 따르고 홀로 사색하며 미진했던 일들을 다시 챙겨보는 자기 성찰도 따르는 계절이기도 하다.

하늘에는 야들한 햇 이불솜을 간간이 찢어 내던진듯한 흰 구름이 무심히 두둥실 떠있는 어느 화창한 날. 난 도심지를 조금 벗어난 한 한적한 가을 길을 달려보았다. 길목엔 가을 풍경이 홍건이 넘쳐난다.

이미 추수가 끝나 누런 가을 빛으로 물든 광활한 들녘에는 초가집채 만하게 말아놓은 건초덩이가 여기저기 무심하게 뒹굴고 있고 한 켠에는 달덩어리 같은 둥글둥글한 황금빛 누런 pumpkin (주로Halloween Day를 앞두고 등장하는 호박) 이 여기저기 자리하고 앉아, 불어오는 바람 따라 한들거리는 억새풀 사이사이로 환한 얼굴들을 내밀고 의젓하게 멋스러운 가을의 정취를 물씬 쏟아내고 있다.

왜 저토록 많은 호박들을 그대로 방치해 두는걸까. 조바심이 났지만 , 농부들은 겨우내 짐승들의 먹이로 다 거두지않고 남겨둔다니 얼마나 푸근한 농부들의 마음인가. 흙을 가까이 하는 사람. 소박하고 욕심없고 따뜻한 농부들의 너그러움에 흠뻑 정이 간다.

가을은 화려한 결실의 계절! 그러나 이 결실은 세월이 흐른다고 그냥 영그는 것이 아니다. 씨앗하나가 열매를 맺기까지 봄, 여름, 그리고 가을에 이르는 자연의 변화도 이겨야하고 씨앗이 땅에 뿌리를 내리고 자라는 자아변신의 아픔도 견디어야 하는 것이다. 우리가 살아가는 것도 자연의 이치와 다를 바 없다,

특히나 우리 이민의 삶을 살아가노라면 어려운 고개가 높고 낮음이 험하고, 힘들때가 얼마나 많은가. 순간순간에 닥치는 어려움을 잘 견디며 좌절하지 말고 열심히 살아간다는것은 행복을 말하는 것이고 기쁨을 말하는 것이 아니겠는가.

열매는 고통속에서 단물이 고여 맺어진다고 한다. 또한 인간이 사는 것이 뭘까. 짧은 사례지만 차 한잔이라도 마시면서 뭔가 대화도 나누고 조금은 여유로움을 가져 보는 삶. 그것이 우리의 정신 세계와 우리의 삶의 질을 높이는 것이 아닐까.

난 가끔 쌀쌀한 가을 밤, 눈이 시리도록 검푸른 밤 하늘을 올려다보며 총총이 떠 있는 별들을 헤이기도하고, 책갈피에 빨갛게 물든 단풍잎을 넣

어 두었던 머언 옛 추억도 꺼내보는 낭만의 가을을 가져 보기도 한다.

무엇이 단풍을 곱게 물들게 하는것인지 모르지만 단풍이 물들면 가을이고 이 가을이 오면 한 해의 끝이 간다는 자연의 순환을 생각하면서, 보람있는 인생의 가을을 맞아 서로서로 친절하게, 성실하게 살아서 보람을 찾는 그런 가을의 노래를 열심히 부르고 또 부르고 싶다.

감사하는 삶

어제만 해도 초여름 같던 날씨가 오늘은 기온이 뚝 떨어져 몹씨 싸늘하다.

추위를 타는 남편에게 두툼한 자켓을 건네며 우리집 귀염둥이 강아지 뽀삐와 모처럼 온 가족이 이른 새벽 산책을 나섰다.

촉촉이 젖은 잔디밭을 밟으며 뽀삐는 발에 닿는 차가움이 싫은지 엄살을 부리느라 동그란 눈에 어리광을 담고 걸음을 주춤거리며 꼬리만 마냥 흔드느라 바쁘다. 나무마다 어린 잎사귀를 달고 집집마다 파란 초록의 정원에 예쁜 꽃들을 피우고 온 동네는 눈송이가 매달리듯 벚꽃은 한껏 부풀어 탐스러운 꽃송이를 활짝 열어놓고 벚꽃축제를 화려하게 펼치고 있다.

우리는 오솔길을 따라 속삭이듯 지저귀는 아름다운 새소리를 들으며 언덕길을 오르고 있었다. 얕게, 그리고 숨쉬는 듯한 물 흐르는 소리가 들린다.

가까이 가보니 졸졸 흘러내리는 물소리 너머에 파릇한 이름 모를 나물들의 새순이 흐르는 물가에 얼굴들을 수줍게 들고 있고 돌부리 틈새에 노랗게 피어난 민들레꽃을 보면서 생명의 기쁨을 느낀다. 그리고 발부리에 채이고 짓밟히면서도 파랗게 살아남은 질경이의 왕성한 생명력에 감탄한다. 생명이란 참 질긴 것이다. 꽃피고 열매 맺는 풀잎 한포기도 자기가 자라는 의미가 있듯 인간이 살아가는 데는 그 나름대로의 의미가 있지 않겠는가.

셰익스피어는 노고지리의 노래를 그림으로 그리려다가 대문호가 되었다지만 나는 어떤 생각으로 오늘 아침 새들의 노래를 듣고 있는 것일까.

뻐근한 양어깨의 세포 마디마디가 기지개를 활짝 켜도록 열심히 돌려주며 걷는다

하나님이 주신 고귀한 삶을 살면서 오늘로 결혼 36주년 기념일이기도 한 우리 부부는 힘들고 어렵기도 했고 보람도 있었던 이민생활 33년을 회상하며 늘 건강 지켜주셔서 오늘을 살게 하시고 살아있음으로 가능성의 의미를 가질 수 있도록 하시는 하나님의 크신 축복에 감사의 눈물이 고이기도 했다.

어린 시절부터 끈끈한 정으로 마음 문을 확 터놓고 의논도 충고도 하면서 서로를 아끼는 친구가 멀리 샌프란시스코에서 날아와 함께 걷기도 하고, 잊을 수 없는 젊은 날의 사진첩을 꺼내 옛 추억을 더듬어 보면서, 젊었을때는 젊음이 인식되지 않았지만 젊음이 가고 난 지금 젊었었구나 하는 깨달음 속에 인생은 홀로 살 수 없다는 것, 누구에게나 어울려 살던 과거가 있고 현재와 미래를 소유하고 살아가는 인생이 아닌가, 논하기도 했다.

삶은 만남의 연속이며 또 만남의 소중함을 아는 것 그것은 삶을 아는 길이라 하지 않는가. 열린 마음으로 모든 것을 순수하게 받아들이며 모든

것에 감사하는 마음으로 주어진 삶 속에 겸손의 꿈을 갖고 살아간다면 아직 우린 젊었고 또한 더 젊게 살아갈 수 있을 것이다.

섬기며 기쁨으로 감사 찬양하며 꿈을 키우는 사람은 또한 행복한 사람이리라.

나의 오빠

오랜 세월을 두고 늘 마음속에 간직한 감사함을 오늘은 속시원하게 마음놓고 얘기하고 싶어진다. 육남매의 장남으로 태어난 나의 오빠 얘기다. 그리 넉넉지 않은 가정에서 태어나 부산 피난시절 모두들 어려운 시기에 어린 나이에 신문배달하며 가족에게 보탬이 되려고 애쓰고 동생들을 끔찍이도 챙겨주던 어린 시절의 기억이 새롭다.

수복 후 서울에 올라온 우리가족. 어린시절의 추억 듬뿍담긴 정들었던 집은 폭격으로 폐허로 변해있었고 마포 공덕동에 한옥을 사서 입주했다. 이 집에서 일어난 가족들의 갖가지 병치레, 6살짜리 남동생이 밖에 나가 놀다가 또래 아이들과 꿀꿀이 죽을 나누어 먹고 체해 이틀을 앓다 그만 우리 곁을 떠났다.

자식이 죽으면 어머니 가슴에 묻는다고 어머니는 식사도 못하시고 점점 몸이 쇠약해지기 시작하니 동네 어른들이 집터가 안좋아서 그러니 이사가라고 야단들이었다. 원효로에 아담한 이층 양옥집을 사서 이사했다. 한창 친구들과 놀기도 바쁜 중학생 오빠는 앞마당에 토끼장, 닭장을 만들어 병아리를 키우며 엄마의 허전한 마음을 달래드리느라 바빴던 그 시절 오빠의 정많은 모습을 그려보는 아침이다.

모든 면에서 뛰어났던 오빠는 졸업후 직장을 갖고 결혼 후에는 따로 살림을 나 살았지만 효심은 변함이 없었다. 갑자기 어머니의 위암 초기 진단은 우리 가족의 큰 충격이었다. 수술하시고 병원에서 요양하실 때 어머니를 바라보는 오빠의 퀭한 눈은 언제나 촉촉이 젖어 있었다

오빠는 큰 제재소를 운영하면서 모든 일이 순조로울 때 수술 후 5년을 잘 지내시던 어머니의 병이 재발되어 수술도 할 수 없다니 청천병력이었다. 오빠는 간호사를 채용해 어머니를 돌보게 하고 새언니는 아예 짐을 챙겨 어머니 곁을 지켰다. 수입품 진통제를 구하느라 백방으로 뛰어다녔고 나중에는 한 시간에도 몇 대씩 맞는 진통제 주사에 성한 곳이 없는 엉덩이를 열심히 소독하는 그 열성은 누가 따를 수 있었을까……

가족의 정성에도 어머니는 다시 올 수 없는 길을 가셨다. 소설에서나 듣던 새엄마가 등장하고 막내 여동생과 남동생은 새엄마와 살기 싫다며 고만고만한 나이의 아이가 넷이나 있는 오빠네 집으로 옮겨가 살았다. 대학 공부시키고 결혼시켜 살림 내고, 미국 사는 동생들이 고국 나들이 할 때면 새언니는 어머니 역할을 싫은 내색 한번 없이 충실히 해준다. 모두들 각박한 세상에 산다지만, 언제나 넉넉한 마음을 지닌 언니가 있다는것이 정말 자랑이고 큰 축복이다.

오빠는 정말 우리집안의 기둥이었다. 젊은 가장으로 아버지 대신 여러 형제들을 자기 자식 같이 사랑하고 엄하게 다스렸다. 요새 같이 의리도 책임감도 헌신짝 같이 버리는 세상에서 나는 우리 오빠를 진실로 존경하고

사랑한다.

만약 그런 오빠가 우리들에게 없었다면 과도기에 우리 형제들은 얼마나 방황 했을까?

그런데 요즘 오빠의 건강이 좋지 않다니 걱정이다. 우리에게 늘 든든한 버팀목이 되어주는 오빠의 건강을 위하여 기도드린다. "힘내세요" 오빠, 언니! 파이팅!!!!

라인 댄스 선생

오늘 난 라인댄스 선생으로 초빙(?)되어 간다.

서둘러야지. 하나 둘 모여든 친구들이 어느새 열두 명. 비지니스를 하는 친구는 종업원에게 가게를 맡기고, 마음좋은 남편님들은 아내를 약속된 장소에 고이모셔다 놓고 가신다. 오랫만에 만남이라, 모두가 상기된 얼굴에 웃음이 가득 피어있다

뷔페식당에서 모인 우린 다양한 음식을 날라다 먹으며 서로의 안부와 쉬지않고 이어지는 대화속에서 중년을 넘긴 여인네들만의 웃음의 파도를 타고 행복한 분위기에 푹 빠진다. 디저트와 커피까지 말끔히 비우고 모임을 주최한 친구집을 향해 모두들 차에 시동을 건다.

여인들로 꽉 채어진 리빙룸은 즐거움에 열기가 뜨겁다.

빨리 라인 댄스를 시작하자고 서두르는 친구들이 마구 선생을 불러대며

야단 법석이다. 여고 시절 고전 무용을 배운적은 있었으나 내가 댄스의 선생이라니 말도 안 된다. 60 평생 제대로 된 춤 한번, 박자 한번 맞춰본 적 없는 , 현대에 한참 뒤쳐진 여자가 지난 번 국제동창회에 가서 장기자랑에 출전하기 위해 배운 라인댄스가 어찌나 재미있던지 댄스 자랑했던 것이 계기가 되어 그만 댄스하고도 선생 자가 붙었으니 오래 살고 볼 일이다.

신나는 음악이 흐르고 4박자를 맞추며 두 줄로 선 12명이 오른쪽, 왼쪽, 뒤로, 앞으로 열심히 발을 옮기기에 바쁘다. 머리 좋은 친구는 어느 새 제 박자를 맞추며 몸까지 유연하게 움직이고, 박자가 제대로 안 되는 친구는 슬쩍슬쩍 고개를 기웃거리며 옆 사람 스텝을 컨닝하며 박자 맞추느라 정신없다.

두어 시간 반복에 반복을 거듭하더니 모두가 기막히게 박자 하나 안 틀리고 빵그르르 갖은 동작으로 멋진 춤 솜씨를 발휘한다. 늦게 배운 도둑이 날 새는지 모른다고 춤바람 나는 것 아닐까 라고 저마다 한마디씩 해서 한바탕 숨넘어가게 '까르르' 웃음파도가 지나간다.

라인 댄스는 추면 출수록 매력 있는 스포츠 댄스의 으뜸. 매일 30분만 열중하면 관절에도 많은 도움이 되고 흔히 일어날 수 있는 중년기의 우울감을 떨쳐버릴 수 있는 좋은 운동, 건강하고 멋진 삶을 살게 될 것이라 생각된다.

어설픈 라인 댄스 선생이되어 멋진 멜로디에 발맞추며 함께 한 즐거움 속에 마구 쏟아내는 앤돌핀이 모두를 10년은 젊게 했으리라.

바닷가에서의 행복

오랜만에 가족이 함께 바닷가로 나들이 가는 날이다.

9인승 밴에 가득 짐을 싣고 풍성한 검푸른 나무숲을 스치며 고속도로를 지나 옥수수밭이 넓게 펼쳐진 시골길을 마냥 달려간다. 미시간에 사는 작은 딸네도 비행기로 머틀 비치를 향해 날아오는 중이다.

가족 캠프장 안에 있는 5베드룸 콘도에 온 가족이 도착해 짐들을 풀며 바삐 움직인다. 난 손자 손녀들과 백사장에 나가 앉아 장난감 삽으로 모래를 퍼 담으며 모래 위에 그림도 그리며 모래성도 쌓고 모래를 깊게 파 고인 물에 조그마한 발들을 담그며 좋아라 깔깔댄다. 물위에 떠서 올려다보는 파아란 하늘에 떠다니는 뭉게 구름이 어찌나 아름답고 평화로운지 마치 선녀가 되어 구름 위를 날으는 기분이다.

사위들이 구워대는 바비큐, 딸들이 만들어 주는 스파게티, 내가 만든 매콤하고 감자 듬뿍 든 닭찜이 집에서 먹을 때와는 전혀 다른 꿀맛이다. 손자 손녀들을 위해 수족관 나들이 갔을 때 아이들이 좋아하는 영화 'Finding Nemo' 에 출연한 물고기들이 모두 모여있어 꼬리 흔들며 헤엄쳐 다니는 것을 보고 큰 어항 벽을 두들기며 신나서 어쩔 줄 모르는 모습을 비디오에다 담느라 사위들이 바삐 움직인다.

해가 지고 사방이 어둑어둑해지면 출렁이는 바다 위에 둥근 보름달이 서서히 떠오른다. 달빛 먹은 바다는 뽀얀 안개를 드리운 듯 찰랑찰랑 조용하고, 그윽한 사랑의 세레나데가 마냥 흘러나올 것 같다. 손자 손녀들이 할머니라고 부를 때만 난 틀림없는 할머니가 된다. 아직 난 철이 덜 들어(?) 바다에 뛰어들어 파도 타는 재미에도 흠뻑 빠지고 아이들이 풀장에 갈 때 남편과 함께 살짝 골프장으로 달려가기도 했다.

매미소리가 정겹고, 이름도 특이한 마녀(The Witch)란 골프장은 유난히 긴 나무다리와 호수가 많았다.

이름 모를 들꽃들이 만발해 꽃동산을 이루고 빼곡이 서 있는 검푸른 소나무 가지위에 신기하게도 하얀 학이 무리 지어 앉아 있었다. 집에 펴놓은 병풍에서나 보던 학을 보고 나도 모르게 감탄사가 나온다.. 어디서 날아왔을까. 환상의 날개를 쭈욱 펴보이며 이 나무 저 나무로 옮겨 다니는 난생 처음 보는 학들, 숲 속에서 별안간 뛰어나와 겁 없이 내 앞에 우뚝 선 엄마 사슴, 아기 사슴의 예쁘고 선한 눈망울들, 두툼한 꼬리를 잽싸게 흔들어 대며 술래잡기하는 다람쥐들, 꺾어질 듯한 긴다리로 여유 있게 서서 물고기를 열심히 노리며 물가에 선 두루미들, 마치 동물의 세계에 와있기나 한 듯 하나님이 펼쳐놓은 자연의 멋진 풍경화에 도취되어 얼마나 행복했는지 모른다

살아 숨쉬며 가족들과 함께 즐긴 바닷가에서의 행복을 추억으로 간직하며, 가족이 하나가 되어 삶의 활력소를 만들고 딸들, 사위들, 손자 손녀들

과 친숙할 수 있는 기회의 소중함을 맛봤다. 매년 가족행사로 이어가겠다는 딸들의 제안에 마음이 흐뭇하고 미소가 가득 채워 진다.

생명의 고마움과 축복

한때 화제를 불러 일으켰던 존 글렌이라는 우주인이 있다.

그는 현재 84세의 할아버지다. 그러나 어느 누구도 그를 할아버지라고 생각하지 않는다. 그는 날마다 실험정신에 불타는 청년이다.

그가 77세에 우주행에 도전했다.

77세 나이에 우주여행을 할 수 있는지 실험해 본 것이다.

물론 그는 성공했다. 지구에 무사히 귀환한 그의 첫 멘트는 다음과 같다.

달력의 나이는 집어치워라! 내 나이는 내가 만든다! 얼마나 파랗고 싱싱한가?

얼마나 자신만만하고 멋진가? 우리라고 존 글렌처럼 살지 말란 법은 없다.

우리도 나이에 연연하지 않는 멋진 삶을 꿈 꾸어보자.

"젊음은 빛나지만 늙음은 고귀한 것." 이렇게 말한 빅토르 위고의 말도 우리는 자주 음미해야한다.

그러나 막상 우리의 현실은 어떤가?

우리 인생의 가을 나이 60대로 들어서게 되면 흔히들 구겨진 은박지처럼 초라해 진다고 한다. 인생이 한편의 영화라면 겨우 나이 60에 아니 벌써 끝 자막이 보여서야.

인생은 60부터가 시작이란다. 멋진 인생의 후반전을 위해서 열심히 살아야 하지 않을까. 우선 우린 건강을 챙기며 지켜야한다. 건강함을 가지고 산다면 얼마나 큰 축복인가.

언젠가 나와 가까이 지냈던 친구가 암투병중에 들려준 말이 생각난다.

그녀가 말하길 사람들은 암환자라면 이미 생명의 의지를 잃어버리고 희미한 눈에 바싹 마른 몸으로 조용히 누워있는 사람을 상상하지만 실제로는 가능한 한 예쁜 옷을 입고 예쁘게 화장하고, 무슨 일이 있어도 병을 이기겠다는 의지로 빛나는 눈을 갖고 있다고 했다.

그녀는 암 투병을 하며 입원실에 하루만 누워있어도 부자나 가난한자나 대학교교수나 국회의원이나 결국 생명이라는 공동의 목적지를 향해 마치 풍랑 속에서 한 배를 탄 사람들처럼 결연한 동지의식을 느낀다고도 말했다. 그리고 그곳에서의 화제는 이전에 관심을 뒀던 것들과는 확연히 다르다고 했다.

누가 어떤 방법으로 돈을 벌었는지, 누가 어떤 자리로 승진했는지, 정치권의 아무개는 왜 그런지, 누구 자식이 어느 대학에 갔는지 등과는 전혀 상관없는 말들로 세상이 다시 그려진다는 것이었다.

그만큼 살고자 몸부림치는 생명 앞에서 돈, 권력, 명예는 초라하고 무력한 것이다.

하나님이 주신 생명의 고마움 잊지 말고 살아야 한다. 그러나 우리는 그 생명의 고마움, 소중함, 위대함, 감격스러움을 자주 잊고 산다.

잘 먹고 소화시킬 수 있다는 것이 그 얼마나 황홀한 경험인지, 자기 두 발로 걸을 수 있다는 것이 세상을 다 얻은 것처럼 위대한 일이며, 자기 두 눈과 귀로 보고 들을 수 있는것이 얼마나 놀랍고 경이로운 것인지 잊고 살기 일쑤다. 결국 살아 있음은 그 자체로 경이로움이요, 감격이요, 황홀이요, 축복이다.

나이 들어감에 연연하지 말고 하나님이 주신 고귀한 삶, 생명의 고마움과 축복 속에서 더 많이 느끼고 보듬고 감격하고 사랑하며 베푸는 삶의 기쁨을 마냥 누리며 열심히 살고 싶다.

설악산 단풍

검푸른 밤하늘엔 초롱초롱 별들이 유난히 반짝이며 밤공기가 으스스 차가움을 더하는 입동이 지난 겨울 초. 여고 졸업반 시절 짝꿍이었던 친구와 팔짱 끼고 깔깔대며 감이 주렁주렁 달린 감나무밭 과수원을 거닐기에 바빴다.

얼마나 잤을까. 어머나! 내가 꿈을 꾼 것인가. 정말 생시 같다. 꿈인게 너무 아쉽다. 친구 생각으로 다시 잠들기가 쉽지 않게 꼬리를 무는데 창문에 드리운 엷은 커튼 사이로 음력 10월 보름달의 밝음이 환하게 비춰주는 깊은 밤이 조화를 이룬다.

설악산 단풍이 곱게 물든 계절에 찾아가기로 한 약속을 어겨서 늘 마음이 어두웠는데 그래도 이렇게 꿈속에서라도 볼 수 있었으니 얼마나 기쁜지…

낮에 편지함을 열었다. 두툼하고 묵직한 누런 봉투가 잡힌다. '물은 답을 알고 있다'는 한 권의 책과 정겨운 편지가 나온다. 글씨도 얼굴만큼 예쁘다.

…처음 동해로 올 적에는 순조로웠는데 이번에는 걸리는 것도 많고 왜 이렇게 복잡한지. 너의 현명한 충고가 많은 도움을 주었으며 힘찬 응원과 위로가 큰 힘이 되어 버틸 수 있었다. 간디의 명언이 생각난다.

"어제 죽은 것처럼 오늘을 살고 영원히 살 것처럼 배우라."

조그만 손거울을 침대 옆에 놓고 수시로 웃으면서 멍청히 보는 버릇이 생겼어. 아상과 아집이 주름살 하나 하나에 새겨질까봐 . 이곳 생활은 산책으로 시작한다. 울산바위와 범바위가 손짓을 하고 다람쥐와 산까치가 마중을 나오는 호수가는 그대로 한폭의 그림이다. 단풍잎과 솔방울을 한웅큼씩 주어와 수북히 쌓아놓고는 '삶은 한바탕 꿈' 이라고 중얼거리며 세상이 어떠한가 보다 세상을 어떻게 볼 것인가를 배운다. 슬픔 뒤에 오는 기쁨이 더 크고 번뇌 뒤에 오는 평화로움이 더 소중하더라.

2003년 달력이 두 장이나 남았는데도 너를 만날 날은 없구나. 2004년 달력은 길고 길어서 너와 만나 보내는 시간도 길고 길었으면 한다…

사랑하는 남편을 잃고 중국으로 인도로 구도의 길을 걷던 친구는 매일 북적대는 도시생활이 싫어 동해바다가 훤히 내려다보이는 고층 아파트에서 3년을 살다가 이제는 정반대로 조용하고 울창한 숲으로 둘러싸인 설악산에 접한 아파트를 사 자연에 묻혀 살고 있다. 나를 위해 크고 작은 예쁜 단풍잎을 주어다 곱게 펴 말려서 조심스럽게 포장해서 책과 함께 보내왔다. 사진틀을 사다 예쁜 설악산 단풍잎을 곱게 끼어 장식해 걸어놓고 친구보듯 보아야겠다.

내년에는 틀림없이 고국 나들이가 이루어져 43년 긴 세월과 오는 세월을 얘기 하리라.

여행중에 만난 사람들

"형님, 수진이가 결혼한답니다."

LA에 사는 손아래 동서한테서 전화가 걸려왔다. 얼마나 기다렸던 기쁜 소식인가. 평소 애리조나주 피닉스로 여행가고 싶어한 남편은 조카 딸 결혼할 때 가자고 미루어왔는데 얼마나 잘된 일인가.

남편은 LA와 애리조나주 지도를 구입해와 열심히 길을 익히고 또 인터넷에 들어가 이것저것을 찾으며 바쁘게 준비했다.

비행기는 캘리포니아를 향해 날아갔다. LA 공항에 도착해서 자동차렌트를 했다. 색깔도 예쁘고 정열적인 빨간색 4도어 세단이다. 남편은 신혼여행을 온 기분이 난다했다. 착각은 자유라던가.

남편이 길 공부를 잘 해놓아 한번도 실수없이 시누이 집에 도착했다.

10여년만에 재회였다. 14년전 남편을 잃고 홀로된 시누이와 늠름하게 장성한 두 조카아들이 대견하기만 했다. 둘이 살기도 힘든 이민 생활인데 혼자의 힘으로 열심히 건강하게 살고 있어 기뻤다.

다음날 오랜 세월만에 만난 남편의 친구 부부는 우리를 위하여 가게문도 닫고 태평양이 내려다 보이는 멋진 골프장으로 초대해주었다. 저편 바다 끝에 걸려있는 붉게 물든 석양이 바닷속으로 꼴깍 숨어들 때까지 우린 골프를 즐겼다. 명쾌한 성격의 이 부부는 옛날과 조금도 변하지 않았다.

조카딸의 결혼 리허설 디너에서 시동생과 동서와의 오붓한 만남의 기쁨을 누리고, 어깨가 확 파진 빨간 드레스를 입은 4명의 들러리에 둘러싸인 눈부신 하얀 드레스를 입은 조카딸, 너무도 예쁜 신부의 야외결혼식이 좋았고 특히나 조카사위의 늠름함이 마음에 든다. 처음 만나는 사돈과의 만남도 낯설지 않았다.

우린 평평하게 펼쳐있는 사막 한 가운데를 갈라서 만들어진 고속도로를 타고 애리조나 피닉스를 향해 마냥 달렸다. 크고 작은 선인장, 벌거숭이 산과 모래들판마다 하늘을 향하여 삐죽삐죽 가시를 뽐내며 신기하게 서 있다. 6시간여를 운전한 끝에 피닉스의 페블 크릭 실버타운(Pebble Creek Silver Town)에 도착했다.

2 Car Garage에 가구도 잘 배치된 2베드름 홈의 골프 카트까지 갖춘 멋진 싱글홈에서의 3박 4일이었다. “이럴줄 알았으면 누구네랑 같이 왔으면 얼마나 좋았을까” 하면서…….

호숫가 군데 군데 서 있는 야자수와 갖가지 모양의 색다른 선인장을 배경으로 펼쳐져 있는 골프장에서 따뜻한 날씨처럼 포근한 미국인 부부와 이틀간 골프를 쳤다. 한여름엔 덥기는 하지만 습기가 없어좋다고 이사오라고 마냥 자랑을 한다.

한국식당을 찾아가 저녁을 먹으며 한인사회 소식도 접할 수 있는 기회도 가졌다.

LA로 돌아오는 길목에 팜스프링스에서 하루를 머물며 2개의 골프장 주인인 한국분을 만나 즐기기도 하고, LA로 돌아와 여학교 때부터 친자매처럼 지내는 친구 집에 머물며 시내관광에 나선 우린 함흥냉면집에서 얼얼한 입맛에 취하고 전통 찻집을 찾아 향기 그윽한 차맛도 보았다.

특히 친구 친정 어머니가 계시는 양로원을 방문했다. 80%가 한국분이라는 이 양로원에서는 한식은 물론 미역국, 냉면까지 메뉴에 들어있고 빨래는 물론 샤워도 도와준다니 얼마나 다행인가.

25년만에 만난 어머니는 팔십을 넘기셨는데도 기억력은 좋으셨지만.

다리에 힘이 없어 보조기를 이용해 걸으신다. 젊어서는 자식들을 위하여 물 불 가리지 않고 헌신하시고 미국에 오셔서는 손자,손녀를 돌보며 자식들을 위해 봉사하셨던 그 건강하셨던 어머니와 많은 노인들이 넓은 현관에 옹기 종기 앉아 방문자들을 바라보는 모습이 나를 슬프게했다.

친구의 어머니가 젊은 시절에 즐겨 부르셨던 '옛날의 금잔디 동산에 메기 같이' 노래를 불러드리니 금방 눈물을 글썽이시며 따라 부르신다. 여행을 끝내고 버지니아에 돌아와서도 유난히 그 어머니의 모습이 떠오른다. '옛날의 금잔디…' 그 노래의 멜로디가 오늘도 내 귀에 들리는 것 같다.

이웃 사촌

45일간의 긴 여행길을 나서게 된 지난 가을이다. 장기간 집을 비워야 하니 여러모로 걱정이 앞섰지만 늘 가까이 지내는 이웃이 있어 다행이었다.

바로 옆집에 사는 스미스 부부다.

4년 전 이 집으로 이사오던날 키가 유난히 큰 백인 부부가 친절하게 다가와 반갑게 인사를 했다. 결혼 10년이 훨씬 넘도록 아기가 없는, 갓 결혼한 신혼부부 같은 잉꼬 부부다. 주말이면 두 손을 꼭 마주잡고 동네를 거니는 다정한 부부, 집 주위를 그림같이 가꾸는 꽤나 부지런한 부부다.

어느 날 함박미소를 지으며 임신했다는 소식을 알려줬다. 얼마나 기뻤는지 눈물까지 글썽였다. Mrs Smith는 51세, Mr Smith는 47세, 늦은 나이에 첫 아기를 가졌으니 얼마나 기쁠까.

몇 달이 지난 어느 날 숨이 넘어가게 달려와 더 기쁜 소식이 있다고 했다. 아들 딸 쌍둥이를 하나님께서 축복해 주셨다며 또 눈물을 보였다.

조그마한 승용차만 타고 다니더니 밴으로 바꾸고, 분주하게 아기용품을 사들이더니 마침내 건강한 아들 딸 쌍둥이를 낳았다. 엄마 아빠가 되었다고 싱글벙글 기쁨을 감추지 못하던 모습이 아직도 눈에 선하다.

나이 들어 처음 아기를, 더욱이 갓난 쌍둥이 아기들을 돌보기가 얼마나 힘들고 바쁠까. 그렇게 말끔히 잘 가꾸던 잔디는 소가 뜯어먹기 좋게 풍성하게 자랐는데도 나 몰라라 엄두를 못 낸다. 남편이 우리 잔디 깎는 날 몇 번 깎아주었더니 고마워 어쩔 줄 모르고 두고두고 땡큐를 연발한다. 유모차에 쌍둥이를 태우고 나오는 날이면 으레 우리 집을 들르는데, 아기들이 방긋방긋 옹알이 하는 모습이 너무나 귀엽다.

장기간 집을 비우게 된다고 하니까 집안에 있는 화초에 물주기, 잔디 깎기, 낙엽 긁기 등 아무 염려 말고 즐겁게 다녀오란다. 서로 믿고 도울 수 있는 이웃이 있어 살아가는 것이 즐겁고, 그들의 싱글벙글 행복한 미소가 있어 이웃인 우리도 행복함에 젖으니 감사하다.

좋은 이웃에게 집을 통째로 맡기고 마음놓고 한국을 거쳐 일본, 중국, 캘리포니아까지 45일간이나 아무 탈없이 건강하게 여행할 수 있도록 축복을 주신 하나님께 감사 드리며 이웃사촌과 오가는 정 속에 뿌듯함이 내 삶에 활력소가 되어 넘친다.

젊은 날의 추억

‘따르릉’ 전화벨이 요란하게 울린다. 한참 잠에 취해 있는데 누구지? 이 이른 시간에 전화기 너머의 목소리의 주인공은 작은 딸이다. 웬일이야, 이 새벽에? 그런데 목소리가 우울하게 축쳐져 있다. “엄마 나 왜 이런지 몰라, 너무 외로워” 이게 무슨소리야? 외롭다니? 나는 그 이유를 차근히 듣기 시작했다.

결혼 후 6년간 아담한 집을 지어 입주하고 자기취향에 맞게 아기자기 잘 꾸며가며 첫째, 둘째 아이를 낳고 이웃들과 동기간처럼 우정을 가꾸며 잘 지냈다. 잘나가던 직장에 불경기로 감원 바람이 불기 시작하면서 사위가 직장을 노스캘로라이나로 옮기게 됐다. 셋째 낳기직전 다행히도 집이 팔리고 아기를 낳자마자 곧 바로 이사하는 힘든 과정에서 동기간 같던 친구들과의 헤어짐, 마음에 드는 집을 헌팅하는 일, 새집을 계약하고 이사하는 육체적으로 힘든 일, 친한 친구들과의 동떨어지는 외로움, 더욱이 사위가 출장 중이라니 이런 조건에 출산 후 홀몬의 불균형까지 겹쳐 복합적 우울증을 갖게 된 것 일 테다. 흔히 산후에 일어날 수 있는 산후우울증, 영어로는 'Baby Blue' 라 부른다 한다.

순간 나는 타임머신을 타고 38년전 나의 젊은 날의 추억속으로 빠져든다.

나는 결혼 후 39일만에 남편이 해외출장지로 떠나 아쉽게도 신혼의 단꿈을 다 꾸지를 못했다. 남편의 빈 자리 대신 시부모님의 극진한 사랑을 받았지만 임신한 몸에 우울증으로 고생한 경험이 있는 터다. 첫 아기를 낳고 8개월이 되어서야 돌아온 남편이었으니, 하루가 멀다고 오고간 그리움의 편지가 큰 위안이었으며 남편없이 지내온 그 긴 세월 속에서도 가족이 있으므로 견딜 수 있었다.

가족이 지니는 의미는 그냥 단순한 사랑이 아니라 지켜봐 주는 누군가가 거기 있다는 사실을 상대방에게 알려주는 것, 바로 정신적인 안정감이 아닌가. 돈도, 명예도, 일도 무엇이라도 가족 말고는 그 무엇도 정신적인 안정감을 갖지 못함을 알았다.

한여름 소낙비를 안고 오는 검은 구름이 태양을 가리고 지나갈 때는 순간적으로 캄캄하다. 그러나 어두움은 한순간이며 다시 밝아온다. 밝음은 길고 어두움은 순간이다. 따라서 순간적인 현실의 그늘을 두려워하지 말고 자기 몫의 삶을 잘 챙겨야 할 것임을 배운 시절이었고 .긍정적이고 진취적인 생각은 우리의 삶을 업그레이드 시켜줌을 깨닫기도 했던 그 시절에 고마워하기도 한다.

인생은 노력이요 노력이 행복을 만드는게 아닐까. 사람 얼굴의 근육은 80개로 이루워졌다는데, 무려 7,000가지의 얼굴표정을 지울 수 있다고 한다.

로마의 철학자 키케로(Cicero)는 "모든것이 얼굴에 있다" 고 하지않는가.

작은 딸네에 가서 몇날을 함께 지내고 돌아왔다. 나의 젊은날의 추억을 들려주며 함께하는 시간속에서 점점 딸의 표정이 밝아짐을 보면서 역시 보듬어주시는 하나님의 극진한 사랑에 감사한다. 우리가 살아가면서 서로서로 사랑이 없으면 우린 날개 부러진 추한 새와 같을 것이다.

우리는 날마다 삶의 자유와 행복을 추구하듯이 서로서로 존중히 여기며 위해주며 살아간다면 얼마나 즐거운 일인가. 어제까지 웃지않던 이에게 오늘 아침 환하게 웃음으로 대해보면 어제 보지 못했던 새 아침이 열릴 것이라 생각하며 나의 젊은날의 추억이 헛되지 않은 밝음에 한껏 미소를 지어본다

텃밭의 즐거움

무더위가 한창 기승을 부리더니 말복, 입추가 지나고나자 더위가 한풀 꺾인 아침, 저녁으로 서늘함이 정말 살맛나는 계절이 돌아온것 같다.

뒷뜰 나무숲속에 매미들의 합창소리가 정겹게 들려오는 오후 한때다.

난 고추를 따러 작으마한 텃밭에 나왔다. 그리 넓지 않은 그저 심심풀이로 하는 소꿉장난과 같은 화초가꾸기 정도의 작으마한 규모의 텃밭이다.

어느 날 야외 피크닉을 마치고 시골 동네로 오는데 각종 모종을 잔뜩 내다 놓고 파는 가정집이 눈에 들어왔다. 남들은 모종을 벌써 심었다는데, 이미 늦었지만 서둘러 심어보자는 바쁜 마음에 차를 세우고 둘러보다 토마토, 고추 모종을 몇 그루 사왔다. 밭농사는 찬찬한 남편몫인데 하고 현관앞 잘 보이는 곳에 말없이 모종들을 놓아두었다.

다음 날 부지런하게도 남편이 어느 틈에 텃밭에 가즈런히 심어놓고는 물뿌리개로 시원스레 물을 뿌려 주고 있다. 또한 토마토, 고추 줄기가 곧게 올라가라고 받침대까지 설치해 놓았다. 얼마전엔 후배네 집에서 부추를 몇뿌리 뽑아와 심어놓았더니 제법 부추의 모양새를 갖추며 파아랗게 소복소복 하늘를 향하여 올라오고 있는 게 아닌가. 정말 희망이 보인다. 난 토마토, 고추 모가 얼마나 자랐나 매일 아침 텃밭에 나가 들여다보는 재미에 푹 빠지고, 덩달아 신난듯 토마토와 고추 모들은 어느 새 쬐끄만 꽃망울을 줄줄이 터트리기 시작한다. 매일 물뿌리개로 물을 주면서 "토마토야, 고추야 우리가 얼마나 사랑하는지 알지? 무럭무럭 자라 바람에 쓰러지지 말고 굳세게 많은 열매를 맺는거야. 마실 오는 토끼가 있으면 빨리 말해야 돼, 절대 안된다고 알겠지……."

어느 새 꽃 밑둥에 좁쌀같은 작은 열매가 맺히는것이 얼마나 신통한지. 어쩌면 하나님은 저 미소한 식물에도 유전자를 주어 하나, 둘, 셋……열매를 맺게 하는지 감사가 절로 난다. 이제는 제법 주먹만한 여러개의 토마토가 주렁주렁 달리고, 꽈리고추는 심심플이 땅콩같이 매끼마다 둘이 먹을 만큼은 실하게 열려준다.

신통한 것은 토마토가 한꺼번에 빨갛게 익는 것이 아니고 하나, 둘씩 따먹기 좋게 서서히 익어주고 있으니 얼마나 기특한가. 그런데 자그마한 텃밭에 무슨 영양분이 있다고 잡초까지도 한 몫 하겠단다. 잡초를 뽑아내다 보면 온통 땀 범벅이 된다. 성경에도 말하지만, 탈무드에도 하나님이 아담에게 "너는 이마에 땀을 흘려야 낟알을 먹을 것이다" 라고 말씀하셨다는 내용이 있다. 기분좋게 흘리는 땀은 삶의 기쁨 그 자체이며 이때의 땀방울은 가장 아름다운 짭짤한 보석이라고 하지 않는가.

자그마한 텃밭을 가꾸며 땀 운운하는 것은 타당치 않은 말이겠지만 텃밭을 가꾸면서 나는 온갖 정성을 들여 농사짓는 농부들의 노고를 생각하게 됐고 그들이 흘리는 땀방울은 진정한 짭짤한 보석임이 틀림없다. 그들은 생계를 위한 절대적인 노력이며 희망일 테니 말이다.

저렇게 정겹게 울어대는 매미소리도 얼마후면 사그러들것이고, 그때쯤이면 귀뚜라미의 처량한 울음 속에서 가을도 문턱을 넘고 있겠지.

이제 뒤늦게 텃밭의 즐거움을 만끽한 난, 내년 봄엔 좀 더 폭을 넓혀 오이, 가지, 호박 모종도 틀림없이 텃밭에 가즈런히 심어보리라 마음 먹어본다.

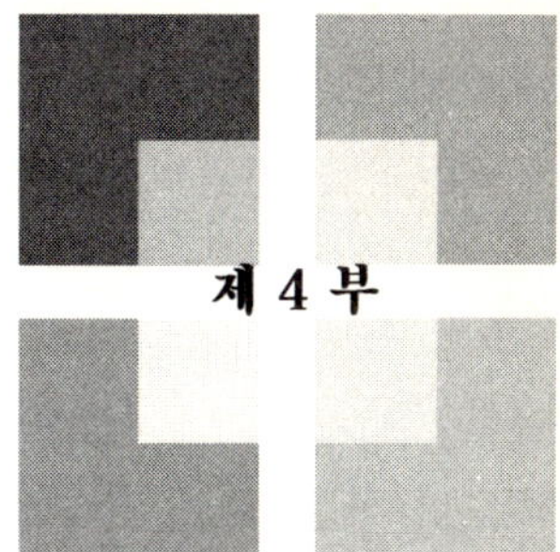

제 4 부

가을 속을 달리는 기차

온 세상을 황금과 붉은 색으로 물들이며 가을 단풍이 절정을 향해 치닫고 있다.

난 바람결에 스며드는 가을빛이 막 나무잎에 찾아와 푸르름이 화려한 단풍으로 변하기 시작할 무렵 뉴욕에서 노스캐롤라이나로 이어지는 앰트랙 79번을 타기위해 알렉산드리아 기차역에 서 있었다.

30분이나 늦장을 부리고도 무슨 벼슬이라도 한양 기차는 '뿌우웅' 기적소리를 요란하게 울리며 역(驛)으로 들어온다. 친절한 승무원들의 안내로 기차에 올랐다. 차창 쪽으로 자리를 정하고 앉자 79번 기차는 역사(驛舍)를 천천히 벗어나며 남쪽으로 달려간다. 장장 8시간 넘게 걸린다는 목적지 Kannapolis 역까지는 열여섯번째 정거장이라니 느긋하게 책 두권과 먹거리는 충분했고, 덜커덩 거리는 기차 안은 좌석이 텅텅 비어 호젓하니 가을 하늘같은 자유함속에 혼자 하는 기차여행도 별난 맛이 있어 좋기만 하다.

힘차게 달려가는 열차에 발맞추듯 가을이 따라오고 있었다. 차창밖으로 푸르른 평야가 신선한 충동감을 안겨주며 황금빛으로 누렇게 변한 들판은 가을햇살을 받아 한 폭의 수채화를 그려내고 있다. 간이역마다 타고내리는 승객들을 바라보며 서민들의 애환이 담긴 얼굴 표정들이 있어서 정답고 호기심이 간다.

청춘은 청춘들대로 나이든 이는 나이든 대로 시간의 흐름을 음미하기에 적격인 계절이다. 청춘은 사랑을 이어갈 것이고 중년의 가을은 추구할 것과 정리할 것을 다듬는 계절이기도 하고, 노년의 가을은 흩어지는 낙엽에 민감하게 받아들일 수 있으나 반면에 지나온 생을 반추하기에 알맞는 계절의 기차여행이 아닌가. 지리함 없이 목적지에 도착했다.

보슬비가 내리는 어둠이 깔린 밤이다. 마중 나온 딸과 만나는 플랫홈의 포옹은 낭만에 흠뻑 젖는 기쁨을 더해준다. 드높은 가을 하늘과 더불어 점점 곱게 단풍이 물들던 날 열흘간의 휴가를 보내고 작은 딸네의 배웅을 받으며 기차에 올랐다.

시야에서 멀어질 때까지 손 흔들며 서있는 딸 가족의 밝은 미소를 보며 진정한 삶의 기쁨과 끈끈한 사랑을 느끼면서도 난 바보같이 눈물이 주르르 흐른다. 소풍가는 아이에게 준비하듯 정성껏 담아준 딸의 점심을 꺼내 먹으면서도 난 왜 이리도 마음이 아릴까. 가까워도 멀어도 가슴 아리게 하는 이별을 대신하듯 기적소리는 여운을 길게 남기며 무심히 떠나간다.

마구 뿌려대던 비도 말끔히 그친 상쾌한 아침에 또한번의 가을 기차여행에 나섰다. 동문들이 함께 웨스트 버지니아로 달려갔다 '포토맥 이글'.기차에 몸을 싣고 단풍진 산허리를 돌며 차창 밖으로 펼쳐진 호숫가 수면엔 푸른 가을 하늘이 깊게 깃들어있고 무리지어 노니는 검정 소들은 냇가 깊은 곳에 그 큰 몸들을 풍덩 담그고 의젓이 앉아있는 모습을 바라보면서 동요로부터 가곡으로 이어지는 분위기는 얼마나 뜨겁고 즐거웠는지. 여고 동창이란 언제나 편안한 분위기를 연출하며 동심의 세계를 넘나들 수 있으니 행복하다.

이제 얼마동안은 철길을 구르는 바퀴소리가 귓전을 맴돌 것이며 가득히 몸속에 앤돌핀을 채우는 풍성함과 결실의 계절속에 마음의 무늬가 아름다운 한 폭의 풍경으로 남아 내 주위의 모든 이에게 짙은 서정을 불러일으키는 사람으로 남고 싶어진다.

눈꽃을 피워놓고 간 친구

어둑어둑 날이 저물고 있다. 커튼을 제치고 밖을 보니 여전 바람 한 점 없이 차분히 내리는 눈이 눈을 시리게 한다. 친구의 고별 예배에는 친구의 사랑하는 남편, 딸, 사위들, 손자들 멀리서 온 친정오빠, 언니 친척들 많은 친지들이 모였다.

생전의 모습이 담긴 사진이 모두를 향해 환하게 웃고 있다. 항상 깔끔하고 예쁜 모습이던 친구는 금방이라도 일어날 것 같은 잠든 모습이 너무나 애처롭다. 사랑하는 엄마를 떠나 보내면서 엄마와의 추억을 더듬으며 준비한 조사를 울먹이며 읽는 딸들의 눈물에 참석한 모두가 울었다.

그와의 추억. 믿음과 구원의 확신이 굳게 서있던 친구. 하와이에 가서 선교훈련 받던 중 의사로부터 병명을 듣고 버지니아로 돌아왔다.

아이를 낳을 때 병원에 간 것밖에는 없었다는 친구는 나이를 거꾸로 먹듯 젊고 늘 미소지으며 깔끔하고 예쁜 모습으로 건강함을 과시했다. 두 달에 한번씩 모여 저녁을 먹으며 자녀들의 얘기, 남편들의 얘기, 미래의 얘기, 특별히 건강관리에 대하여 시간가는 줄 모르고 떠들어대던 동기동창 모임에서 제일로 젊어 보였고 조용하면서도 얘기를 시작하면 모두에게 웃음을 선물해줄 줄 알던 멋진 친구였다. 오랜 세월동안 꽃가게를 운영하며 예쁘게 만들어 내는 꽃바구니에 마음을 담아 갖가지 행사에, 결혼식에 정성을 쏟았었다

떠나기 두 주 전 병원에 찾아간 나를 보고 초췌한 모습으로 처음으로 눈물을 보였다. 열흘 후에 있을 작은딸 결혼식때는 한복을 입어야겠다고 했다. 건강했더라면 결혼식장을 멋지게 꽃장식하고 예쁜 드레스에 화사한 미소로 축하객을 맞이했을 친구는 결혼식에 참석하지 못했다.

딸만 셋을 둔 행복한 엄마였다. 친구 부부는 바쁜 생활속에서도 시간을 내어 여행을 즐기던 잉꼬부부였으며 작년 여름엔 딸들을 데리고 '알래스카'로 멋진 크루즈 여행을 다녀오기도 했다.

전화벨이 울린다. 친구 남편의 목소리다. 가슴이 철렁 소리를 낸다. 조금 전 온 가족과 목사님이 지켜보는 가운데 조용히 눈을 감았단다. 할 일도 많은 아까운 나이에 이렇게 빨리 가다니 너무 너무 마음이 아프고 슬프다. 친구는 떠나기 전날 밤 뜬눈으로 밤새도록 혼자 얘기했단다. 투병중에 늘 말한 대로 60평생을 건강을 지켜주신 하나님께 먼저 감사기도 드렸을 것이고 두고 가는 사랑하는 남편에게 큰딸, 작은 딸, 막내딸에게 하고 싶은 많은 얘기였을 것이다. 친구가 가장 좋아하는 찬송가 98장 '주 예수 내가 알기 전 날 먼저 사랑했네' 찬송 속에 친구는 천국에 갔다.

16년 긴 세월 동안 아름다운 꽃과 생활하던 친구는 마지막 가는 길에도 하얀 눈(雪)꽃을 피워놓고 갔다. 아픈 마음, 천국에서 다시 만날 소망으로 슬픔을 달랜다.

오솔길

'우당탕' 천둥소리가 요란하다. 이른 아침 햇볕을 보여주던 날씨가 후두둑 빗소리를 내더니 유리창을 타고 흘러내리는 빗줄기가 묵은 먼지 때를 말끔히 씻어내면서, 천둥과 세찬 바람을 동반하고 사정없이 쏟아부어대며 무섭게 흘러내리고 있다.

뒷뜰에 서 있는 아름드리 나무들이 세찬 바람에 밀리어 이리저리로 마구 흔들어대며 혹시나 뿌리째 뽑혀 넘어가지나 않나 사실 겁도 난다. 아스팔트 위를 휩쓰는 폭우가 마치 작은 강을 순식간에 만들어 놓더니 빗줄기가 시들해지면서 햇볕이 살짝 얼굴을 내밀며 점점 바깥 공기가 환해지기 시작한다. 5월 한달 거의 매일이다시피 내린 비에 이젠 제발 사정하지만 6월이 들어서서도 햇볕을 보여주는 날이 그리 많지 않다

날씨 좋는 날은 어찌나 더운지 마치 한여름이 성큼 다가온 양 잠시 밖

에 나갔다오면 송글송글 땀방울이 옷을 적시며. 에어콘 소리가 집집마다 요란하다. 텃밭에 심어놓은 고추모가 자라지 못하고 어린 고추모가 그대로 시들해 있고 곱게 정리해 심어놓는 꽃나무들도 이맘때면 화려하게 제 실력을 발휘할텐데 거무튀튀하게 축 처져 있다.

비가 그치고 햇볕이 나오면서 기분 좋게 날씨가 화창해졌다. 난 강아지를 데리고 산책길에 나섰다. 늘 같은 코스를 걷는데 숲이 우거진 길옆에 낯선 조그마한 내리막길이 눈에 들어온다. 그토록 많이 오가던 코스인데 눈에 띄지 않던 길이기에 호기심에 그 길로 발걸음을 성큼 옮겼다. 양쪽으로 우거진 검푸른 나무숲들이 아늑하게 나를 감싸 안는다. 마치 정글에 들어가는 듯 축 처진 나무가지를 젖혀가며 촉촉이 이슬도 내리고 으시시함마저 감돈다.

군데군데 쓰러져 있는 통나무는 썩은 속을 새커멓게 드러내고 연두색을 띤 잔잔한 이끼들이 카페트 모양 오솔길 양옆에 깔려있다. 한참을 걸어 들어가니 저 켠에 자그마한 다리가 보인다. 발걸음을 재촉하며 뛰다시피 가까이 가보니 제법 멋을 내어 지어진 나무다리가 든든하게 개울물을 가로질러 있다. 다리 위에 올라 개울물을 내려다보니 울퉁불퉁한 크고 작은 돌멩이들이 흐르는 물줄기를 방해하듯 어지럽게 널려있고 흐르는 개울가에 이름 모를 풀들이 노란색 보라색 꽃잎을 피워놓고, 뿌리를 송두리째 드러낸 큰 나무들의 뿌리가 계속 흐르는 물에 씻기고 있다.

나는 다리 위에 서서 사방을 두리번거리며 잃어버린 것을 찾기나 하듯 한참 허둥댔다. 옛 추억을 끌어올리며 아주 어린 시절 오빠와 친구들과 개울가에 나가 물장구치며 엉성한 그물로 송사라를 잡던 천진스런 개구쟁이들의 놀이며 엄마 따라 개울가에 가서 빨래하던 어리광 부리던 그 시절도 떠올리게 했다. 다 자라서는 서울 근교에 있는 정릉에서, 자문밖에서, 송추에서 졸졸 흐르는 개울가에서 구두를 벗고 시원한 물에 발을 담그고 젊음을 자랑하며 행복에 젖었었다. 지금 생각하면 싱겁기 한이 없는 일인 것만 같은데 그때의 만남은 마냥 마음을 설레게 하고 만나고 헤어질 때면 아쉽고 다음 만날 날을 손꼽던 그날들이 먼 추억속에 어렴풋이 떠오른다.

난 오늘 아침 그 옛날을 추억하며 우연히 발견한 낭만이 깃든 이 오솔길에서 신선한 공기를 흠뻑 마시며 힘차게 걸을 수 있는 건강주시고 공허해 지려는 마음속에 늘 기쁨으로 채워 주시는 하나님께 감사하지 않을 수 없다. 난 이제 이 오솔길을 따라 남편과 함께 걸으며 힘들고 어렵기도 했고 보람도 있었던 모든 이민생활 30년을 회상하며 잘 성장하여 결혼한 딸들과 사위들의 얘기며 손자, 손녀들의 귀여운 재롱들을 얘기하면서 걸으련다. 더욱이 앞으로 남은 여생 하나님께서 하락하시는 생명 삶 안에서 더욱 보람있고 후회 없는 삶이 되도록 설계하며 노력하면서 다정하게 낭만이 가득한 이 오솔길을 따라 걷고 또 걸으리라.

선배 언니와 잊지 못할 추억들

바람 한 점 없이 무덥던 오후가 지나 어둠이 깔리면서 총총히 반짝이며 빛을 발하던 별들은 시커먼 구름에 가려 보이지 않는다. 무성하게 훌쩍 커버린 검푸른 나무 잎사귀 속에 깃들어 잠자리를 준비하던 새들의 구슬 구르는 예쁜 새소리가 유난히 오늘밤 내 마음을 슬프게 한다.

사랑하는 선배 정우순 언니의 장례식이 꿈 같기만 한데….

갑자기 우당탕 벼락치며 후두둑 후두둑 굵은 빗소리가 지붕을 친다.

사랑하는 언니를 떠나보내는 모든 사람들의 눈물인가 보다. 그렇게도 명랑하고 능동적이고 적극적이며 만능재주꾼으로 어느 모임이든 구석구석을 챙기며 헌신적인 모범을 보여주고, 무슨 음식이든 최고의 맛을 내어 만인의 입을 즐겁게 해주던 일류 요리사 언니. 한국인의 긍지를 살리며 고전무용을 2세들에게 열성적으로 가르치던 전 워싱턴 한인무용단장이셨다.

근 일년 전 캐나다 토론토에서 가졌던 국제동창회 준비를 위해 밤잠도 설치며 수십년 전에 입었던 교복을 입고 이웃학교인 용산고등학교 교복을 한국에 있는 방송국으로 부터 빌려와 여고시절을 재연하며 '어느날 여고시절 우연히 만난 사람'과 '아 옛날이여'를 열창하며 장내가 떠나가도록 아낌없는 박수를 받았던 그 기발한 아이디어는 언니만이 연출할 수 있는 작품이었다.

선후배가 짙은 코발트색 모자 달린 우비들을 입고 나이아가라 폭포 물줄기가 펑펑 쏟아 붓는 데까지 유람선에 실려서 온통 폭포물을 뒤집어쓰고 예쁘게 피어 오르는 무지개를 바라보며 흠뻑 젖은 옷을 말릴 겨를도 없이 즐거워하는 우리의 모습을 사진에 담기에 바빴던 언니, 한국 식당을 기어코 찾아내 맛있는 생선찌개를 가운데 놓고 나누어 먹던 일, 미끄러지듯 흘러가는 유람선을 타고 그 많은 천 개의 섬을 돌던 즐거운 시간들이며 선후배가 골프를 치며 즐기던 그 시간들이 이제는 다시 올 수 없는 먼 추억으로 가고 있다. 더 잊지 못할 것은 월드컵 4강 진출의 꿈을 안고 한국의 남아들이 펼치는 경기를 토론토 한 호텔 방에서 언니가 준비해온 빨간 티셔츠를 하나씩 나누어 입고 밤을 홀딱 새어가며 목터져라 응원했던 그 밤을 영원히 잊지 못한다.

어느 날 다리가 아프다며 양팔에 목발을 짚고 나타나셨다. 신경통인가 봐 하시며 이민 100주년 행사를 돕던 언니. 더 늙기 전에 할 수 있는 일이면 열심히 해야겠다는 의욕을 보여준 언니. 투병중에도 흐트러짐 없이 매사를 꼼꼼히 챙기며 심지어는 마지막 가실 때 입고 갈 한복도 손수 찾아 준비해 놓고 고별예배 때 비치해 놓은 사진도 사진틀에 곱게 끼워놓는 여유있는 분. 예쁜 딸들에게 엄마가 아끼며 소장했던 그림과 가구 등 아끼던 물건들을 골고루 원하는 대로 공정하게 분배해 놓으셨던 딸만 넷을 두었던 언니. 오늘 어머니날을 맞아 네 딸들은 엄마 생각으로 얼마나 많은 추억을 떠올리며 많은 눈물을 쏟을까 가슴이 뭉클해진다.

서울대 동창회에서도 수도여고 동창회에서도 큰 보물을 잃었다. 잔잔한 미소를 머금은 예쁜 모습과 알맞은 몸매를 완전히 숨긴 채 운구차는 앞장서서 움직이고 뒤따라 유족들이 탄 긴 하얀 리무진 2대가 뒤따르고 헤드라이트를 켜고 친구, 친지, 동창선후배가 줄지어 잘 정리된 파란 넓은 잔디 위에 온갖 색깔의 아름다운 꽃들이 만발한 장지 정문을 들어서는 모습이 마치 언니가 천국문에 들어서는 것 같아 보였다.

언니가 작년 제 생일 선물로 준 예쁜 브로치가 나를 보고 웃고 있네요. 언니를 뵙듯 아끼며 제 옷에 장식할 겁니다. 아픔이 없는 천국에서 못다한 행복을 영원히 누리실 것을 믿으며 선배언니와 잊지 못할 추억들을 기억하며 다시 만날 소망을 굳게 갖고 슬픔을 달랩니다.

벚꽃 속의 봄방학

전국이 꽃잔치로 들썩인다. 온통 개나리, 수선화가 꽃망울을 활짝 열고 온 동네를 노랗게 물들여 놓았고, 눈부시도록 하얀 꽃들이 흐드러지게 피어나 황홀하기 그지없다.

몇 달 전부터 봄방학하면 할머니집에 나들이 온다고 손꼽던 8살, 5살의 손녀딸들이 고대하던 봄방학을 맞아 엄마 따라 나들이 왔다. 오자마자 익숙하게 제집인양 이층으로 올라가 방 하나씩 차지하고 옷가지며 인형들을 챙겨놓느라 한참 부산을 떨고는 리치몬드 집으로 돌아가는 엄마를 향해 무심하게도 '빠이' 하며 손 한번 흔들어주는 천진난만한 아이들의 모습을 본다.

떠들고 뛰노는 아이들의 세계 속에 조용했던 집안 곳곳에 활력이 넘쳐난다.

첫날은 수영장으로 갔다. 큰손녀딸은 수영에 자신 있다고 덥석 물속으로 풍덩 뛰어들고 작은아이는 수영이 서투르니 고무풍선을 양팔에 끼고 물장구치며 오리처럼 수영장을 헤매며 좋아라 깔깔댄다.

다음날은 할아버지가 준비해둔 연을 날리기 위해 가까운 동네공원으로 달려갔다. 아이들이 좋아하는 인형 'DORA' 얼굴로 가득 채워진 연은 하늘 드높이 올라 불어대는 바람 따라 이리저리 하늘을 휘젓고 있고 아이들의 마음도 저 높이 떠 있는 연을 타고 흥분에 들떠 있다. 컴퓨터게임에 익숙해 틈만 있으면 내 컴에는 작은아이가, 할아버지 랩탑에는 큰 아이가 독차지하고, 마음에 드는 DVD를 넣고 빼는 일에 주저 않는 솜씨에 놀란다.

잠자리에 들기 전 한차례씩 발레 춤을 선보이는데 활달한 큰손녀가 리드하고 작은 손녀는 하고 싶어 하면서도 막상 멍석을 깔아주면 꼬리를 내리는 부끄럼쟁이, 조개처럼 입을 꾹 다물고 침묵을 흘릴 때도 많고 울기도 잘한다.

파란 하늘엔 뭉개구름, 새털구름을 만들어내며 각양 각색의 형태들로 참으로 매혹적인 화창하고 따사로움이 그지없는 아침이다, 긴 여행이 아닌 가벼운 하루 나들이 명목으로 손녀딸들과 벚꽃축제가 열릴 워싱턴DC로 달려간다. 차창 밖 봄꽃들이 예쁘게 손짓하는 흥겨움속에 손녀들과 속삭임을 나눌 수 있는 공간이 즐겁기만하다. 다시 한 번 내 가족, 내 이웃, 내 사랑이 참으로 소중함을 느끼며 꽃이 지기 전에 감추어 두었던 나의 사랑을 마음껏 나누어 주어야겠다.

분명 봄은 자연의 순리를 말보다 행동으로 생명을 노래하고 사람들에게 화해와 용서와 그리고 절망에서 희망를 노래하는 신비로운 힘을 갖게 하는 사랑의 계절인 것 같다. 백악관, 링컨기념관, 제퍼슨기념관, 워싱턴 모뉴먼트, 국회의사당을 들러보며 좋아라 하고, 핑크빛으로 화려하게 만발한 벚꽃축제로 인산인해를 이룬 호숫가를 손을 꼭 잡고 걸으며 환하게 웃는 모습들을 디카에 담느라 할아버지도 엄청 바쁜 하루였다.

아이들의 미소처럼 벚꽃의 향기와 지워지지 않은 사랑의 향기속의 추억을 만들며 화사한 벚꽃 무더기보다 더 붉은 열정으로 일주일동안 봄방학을 함께한 손녀딸들과 행복한 마음을 언제까지나 간직하고 싶어진다.

새싹이 움트는 봄

자연은 신비 그 자체, 누가 뭐라 하지도 않지만 어김없이 긴 겨울의 끝자락을 들치면서 어느 틈엔가 봄은 소리 없이 우리 곁에 서서히 다가오고 있다. 계절의 선율을 타고 겨우내 외로이 벌거벗었던 나무가지마다 이제 물이 올라 생기가 돌고 쬐그마한 망울들을 매달았는가 하면 축 늘어진 수양버들도 연녹색으로 물들이며 산뜻한 봄의 향연을 펼칠 준비가 한창이다.

그 옛날 어린 시절 앞마당에 암탉이 노오란 병아리들을 몰고 도란거리던 소리며, 우물가에서 빨래하는 방망이질 소리, 골목 안을 활기차게 하는 아이들의 뛰노는 소리가 이때가 되면 추억의 한 귀퉁에 머물며 마냥 그리워지는 계절이기도 하다.

늦은 밤부터 내리기 시작한 봄비가 대지를 흠뻑 적셔 놓았고 며칠째 세차게 불어대던 바람도 잠재운 화창한 아침이다.

난 갑자기 궁금증이 생겨 겨우내 무심했던 텃밭으로 가본다. 한 여름 내내 식탁의 한자리를 차지하며 입맛을 돋워 주었던 부추, 작년 가을에 밑둥만 남기고 싹뚝 짤라주었는데 기특하게도 차가운 땅을 열고 연초록 얼굴들을 쏘옥쏘옥 내밀고 폼을 내고 있고, 뒷뜰엔 지난 늦가을 쑥 몇 뿌리를 캐다 심어놓았는데 얼어 죽지않고 신통하게도 여기저기에 파아란 잎새를 줄줄이 펴내고 있지 않은가 .이제 조금만 기다리면 무성하게 자란 쑥잎을 따서 데치고 믹서에 갈아서 몸에 좋다는 쑥떡을 만들어 먹을 수 있으리라.

지난해 준비해 두었던 씨앗들을 찾아 놓았다. 앞마당 한 귀퉁이를 파내고 꽃씨라도 심어보고 싶고 텃밭에는 오이, 가지, 고추 같은 씨앗을 심고 싶은 마음이 성급해지니 너무 이른 걸까. 씨앗을 준비하지 않아 봄을 헛되이 보낸다면 일 년 내내 아름다운 꽃구경은 물론이지만 한여름에 물조리개로 시원하게 물 뿌려주면 방긋방긋 웃으며 실하게 자란 고추며 토마토를 따먹는 솔솔한 재미는 어쩔 것인가.

새싹이 움트는 봄이라는 계절의 축복과 우리들의 땀이 밴 노력만이 한 해를 더욱 풍성하게 만들 것이라 생각되는 계절이기에 희망이 보인다. 골프장에도 날씨에 민감해 카트를 타고 공을 날리는 썸들로 붐빈다. 골퍼들의 발자국에 놀라 모처럼 봄나들이 나온 거북이와 자라는 겁에 질렸나 재빨리 연못 속으로 풍덩 숨어드는 모습이 안스러워 한참을 연못 속에서 시선을 떼지 못했다.

모든 만물이 기지개를 켜는 봄의 내음 속에 약동의 계절임이 분명하다. 추운 겨우내 움추려 들었던 몸과 마음을 활짝 펴고 큰 날개짓으로 하늘높이 비상하는 독수리 처럼 더 높이 더 멀리 날아오르기를 소원하며. 이 봄부터 모두의 마음밭에 사랑의 꽃이 활짝 피었으면 좋겠다. 나무마다 새싹이 움트는 소리, 꽃나무마다 꽃망울 튀우는 소리, 바야흐로 생동의 계절을 맞아 그 동안 잊고 지냈던 잠재된 사랑이 다시 기지개를 켜는 활기찬 일상으로 나아가리라.

아찔했던 그 순간의 추억

그러니까 지난 해다. 여행자들을 공격한다는 집시들의 출몰에 조심하라는 가이드의 엄한 지시에 따라 조심하며 터키의 성지 곳곳을 여행 할 때였다.

그러던 어느 날, 한 호텔에서 그만 여권과 돈이 든 핸드 백을 몽땅 잃어버리는 기막힌 사건이 터지고 말았다. 일행들과 호텔식당에서 저녁을 먹고 자리를 일어서는 순간이다. 옆에 나란히 앉아서 식사했던 일행 한 분이 먼저 자리를 뜨며 재킷을 두고 갔다.

'어머나 재킷을 두고 갔네' 하는 순간 '어머! 내 핸드백은?'

식탁 밑 의자 앞, 뒤, 옆을 암만 찾아봐도 그림자도 없다. 정말 큰 일이 아닌가.

가슴이 쿵 쿵 소리를 내기 시작한다. 심장이 멎는 것 같다.

가만 가만 생각을 더듬으며 호텔 방에서 나올 때를 기억 속에서 끌어내 봤다. 핸드백이 무거워 선글래스, 카메라, 이것저것을 꺼내놓고 들고 나온 게 분명하다.

내 딴엔 내 품에 있어야 안전 할 수 있다고 생각해서 꼭 내 옆구리를 지키게 했는데 아차, 그래, 거기다 두고 온 거야. 한 시간 전 3층에서 일행들과 커피를 마셨던 그 곳이다. 마구 떨리는 마음으로 허둥대며 3층으로 뛰어 올라갔다. 이미 불은 꺼져있고 아무리 둘러봐도 찾을 길이 없다.

이를 어쩌지. 여행이고 뭐고 온 몸에 힘이 쭉 빠져 주저앉을 것 같다. 후들거리는 걸음으로 난간을 붙잡고 층계를 내려오다 저 켠에 몇몇 사람들이 앉아서 술 마시는 '바' 가 확 눈에 들어온다. 커피 룸에서 우리에게 커피를 서브 해주던 터키 아가씨가 있지 않은가. 난 황급히 다가가 "실례합니다. 저 기억하세요? 한 시간 전 3층 커피 룸에서 핸드백을 잃어버렸는데요" 내 목소리는 분명 울음 섞인 처량한 목소리였을 것이다. 그 아가씨는 환한 미소를 띠면서 "검정 핸드백이지요? 프런트 데스크에 가 보세요, 거기 있을 겁니다" 했다. 소리 없는 환호성을 질러대며 프런트 데스크로 달려 갔다.

저 켠에 검정 내 핸드백이 얌전하게 방긋 웃고 있다. 잘 생긴 청년이 핸드백에 달린 이름 택과 내 말에 일치함을 확인한 후 핸드백을 내준다. 얼마나 얼마나 감사하던지. 백을 열고 여권부터 잘 계신가 챙겨봤다. 돈도 다 그대로다. 난 터키나라가 갑자기 구세주 같이 느껴지며 눈물이 핑 돈다. 너무 고마운 사람, 고마운 나라 터키. 남편한테 정신을 어디다 두고 다녔느냐고 구박 흠뻑 받고, 여행 끝날 때까지 '핸드백 잘 챙기세요' 란 유행어를 만들었다.

한 나라 아니 한 국민 개개인이 베푸는 정직, 친절, 미소와 감사가 어우러져 외국인에게 진정 고마움이 전달되는 과정 과정에서 그 나라를 진단하게 되는 게 아닐까. 때때로 지나쳐간 아찔했던 그 순간의 추억속에 머물때면 정직함과 친절의 나라 터키, 터키인들의 앞날에 무궁한 발전과 하나님의 크신 축복이 함께 하기를 기도한다.

조카딸의 배낭여행

북유럽 여행을 마치고 돌아오는 날과 조카딸이 모처럼 워싱턴을 찾은 날이 공교롭게 겹쳤다. 우리의 공항 도착시간과 조카의 도착시간이 겹치다 보니 리치몬드에 사는 큰딸이 사촌(조카딸)을 마중 나가고, 공항에서 짐을 찾아 곧 바로 한국 식당에서 만나자고 약속했다.

고국 나들이 때면 언제나 시동생네 집에서 묵으면서도 조카딸이 대학 조교로 일하며 공부하느라 늘 늦은 시간에 들어오니 함께 할 시간이 없었는데 이번엔 한참을 친해야겠다고 마음을 다잡았었다

조카딸 혼자서 4개월간 두루두루 다녀온 배낭여행담은 정말 흥미로웠다. 태국, 캄보디아, 베트남, 라오스, 말레지아, 싱가포르의 유명한 곳곳을 배낭여행하기 위해 1년 전부터 가이드북을 사다놓고, 인터넷을 통하여 세밀히 공부에 노트까지 해가며 열심히 준비를 했단다.

여행경비는 매달 받는 월급에서 80%를 꼭꼭 저금해 충분히 자금을 마련하고 셀폰은 해외에서도 국제전화가 가능한 것으로 시스템을 바꾸고, 백팩은 20파운드를 넘지 않게 요령껏 꼭 필요한 옷가지를 넣고, 자그마한 백팩을 하나 더 앞으로 목에 다 걸어 물병과 지도를 넣어 핸드백으로 이용했단다. 최소한의 경비로 최대의 효과 여행을 위해 유스 호스텔을 이용하고 국경을 넘을 때는 비행기보다 10분의 1의 절약형 버스를 이용했는데 베트남에서 라오스로 이동시 탔던 버스는 상상을 초월,. 버스 안 뒷 켠엔 짐이 3분의 1을 차지했고, 거기다 발 디딜 틈도 없이 사람과 닭과 염소까지 겹쳐 함께 국경을 넘는데, 고약한 땀 냄새와 짐승들의 배설물까지 범벅이 되어 지독한 악취 속에서 24시간동안 버티느라 얼마나 고생을 했는지 라오스에 도착하고 이틀이나 심하게 앓았단다.

버스를 택한 자신이 분통이 터지고 바보스러웠지만 지구의 한 켠엔 이런 삶도 있음을 체험하며, 경험의 무대를 넓힘에 감사하기도 했단다.

잊을 수 없는 추억의 사진첩을 겹겹히 채워가며 첵크해놓았던 동남아 명승지를 빼놓지 않고 관광하면서 입맛이 까다롭지 않아 체력 유지에는 별지장이 없었단다.

내친 김에 미국에도 가봐야지 하는 욕심이 발동해 태국에서 미국 LA로 와서 서부 관광과 디즈니랜드, 유니버셜 스타디움을 두루 관광하고, 카나다 토론토, 퀘벡, 나이아가라, 뉴욕의 브로드웨이에서 뮤지컬도 2편이나 관람하는 낭만을 흠뻑 누렸단다.

미국 여행 경비는 부모님이 많이 도와 주었다며 귀국하면 열심히 일해서 갚아야겠다고 환하게 웃으며 떠나가는 조카딸을 배웅하며 모험적인 4개월간의 배낭여행은 젊었기에 가능한 것, 젊었을 때 한껏 누려본 산 경험의 지평이 넓어져 앞으로의 삶에 많은 보탬이 되리라. 역시 젊음이 보배이며 자랑이다.

진정으로 행복해야 할 삶

한밤중이다. 세상은 더없이 고요한데 문득 비가 내리는 듯 하여 잠시 읽던 책을 덮고 살짝 커튼을 젖혀보니 과연 눈앞에 습기가 가득하다. 내친김에 아예 커튼을 헤치니 가을밤 비가 내리는 뒷뜰의 단풍잎들은 바람에 밀려 떨어지는 경치가 사뭇 눈에 감긴다. 온통 떨어진 낙엽들은 '쏴아' 소리를 질려대며 이리저리 뒹구는 아름다운 늦가을의 풍경을 펼쳐내고 있다. 며칠 전 비오는 날 운전대를 잡고 달리는데 이게 웬일? 마구 쏟아지는 비와함께 가벼운 눈을 얹고 차창을 두들긴다.

벌써 겨울이 오는 것일까. 갑자기 아득히 지난쳐간 추억 속에 진한 우정을 간직한 사람. 20대 초반 같은 교회의 주일학교 반사로써 봉사하며 함께 수양회도 다녀오는 수많은 추억 속에 머물게 하는 다정함이 생각난다. 강원도 평창의 어느 마을에 함께 봉사 나가 뽕나무 잎에 누에가 우글대는 방에서 밤을 지새우며 신앙을 논했던 꿈 많던 시절, 난 그녀의 올케로 결혼했고, 남편이 멀리 외국 출장 중에는 시누이 올케가 격이 없이 한방을 쓰며, 우중충한 날씨에 비와 눈까지 범벅으로 뿌려대던 날이면 김치를 송송 썰어 넣고 김치빈대떡을 부쳐 먹으며 깔깔대던 젊은시절이 있었다.

세월은 쏜살같이 어느새 우리를 중년에서 노년으로 내몰고 있다. 가끔 외롭겠다는 나를 시내 다방으로 불러내 함께 차를 마시며, 먹거리로 유명한 집을 찾아 저녁을 먹고 영화를 감상하러 다녔던 일, 마음 넉넉함을 가진 막내 시누이는 새언니가 힘들다고 집안일을 도와주는데도 열심이었다. 손재주가 좋아 조각품을 만들어 벽에 걸어놓은 그 수많은 작품들이 눈에 선하다. 독일에 간호원으로 취업해 가있는 동안 우린 미국으로 이민왔고 시누이는 독일에서 귀국해 결혼해서 첫아이를 낳았을때 우리는 재회의 기쁨을 가질 수 있었다. 그런데 그 착한 시누이에게 큰 슬픔이 닥쳤다.

19년 전 사랑하는 남편을 갑자기 병으로 잃고, 어린 아들 둘을 데리고 막막한 세월 속에서 고민하다 미국 LA로 이민 왔다. 이민생활이란 부부가 함께 뛰어도 여러움이 많은데 언제나 긍정적이고 진취적인 생각 속에 자기가 선택한 이민의 삶을 꿋꿋이 이겨내며 지금껏 밤낮을 가리지 않고 열심히 앞만 보고 살고 있다.

덴탈랩에서 치기공을 습득해 안정된 기술인으로 희망을 가꾸었고 대학원생인 아들은 어머니께 효도하는 장한 아들로 성장해 꿈을 펼치고 있다. 지금도 동터오는 아침을 맞으며 직장으로 향하는 발걸음을 늦추지 않고 바로 사는 삶을 증거하고 있으며 자신의 생활 속에 있는 작은 것들을 소중히 여기며 분수에 맞는 생활이 바로 행복이란다. 행복은 결코 무지개처럼 찬란한 대상이 아니라 행복은 평범하고 작은 일상의 일들 속에 있음을 알기에 진정으로 행복해야 할 그의 삶이 절대로 헛되지 않기를 기도한다.

어려움 속에서도 삶이 가치 있는 것이라 믿는 이야말로 행복한 사람일 것이며, 손마디가 굵어지도록 일한 보람은 누가 보람 있다고 소리쳐서 얻어지는 것이 아니라 스스로 정직하게 살아왔다는 자긍의 세계에서 찾아지는 것이리라.

추억을 불러 준 테입

게으름을 부리는 것도 한정이 있었는지 오늘은 차분히 앉아서 리빙룸 한 쪽 벽에 묵직하게 자리 잡고 있는 옥돌장 서랍 속에 있는 물건들을 하나 둘 꺼내기 시작했다.

이제는 웬만하면 과감하게 정리해야겠다고 마음에 다짐을 하면서 우선 수북히 꺼내놓은 비디오 테입과 카세트 테입부터 붙여져 있는 제목 따라 골라낸다.

유난히 '1994년 4월 20일 형제 모임' 이란 제목을 내 필적으로 쓴 카세트 테입이 눈에 쏙 들어온다. 잘 쓰지 않던 카세트 플레어를 꺼내 먼지를 털어내고 테입을 깊이 밀어 넣었다. 친정 동생들과 온가족이 함께한 가족애가 넘쳐나는 남편의 생일날이었다. 마침 이민을 앞두고 미국견학 겸 방문 온 여동생, 막내 남동생과 수년 만에 가져보는 행복한 순간들이 실려

있다.

누구나 일정부분 삶에서 옛 추억을 담고 살아간다. 이산가족이 된 우리 형제는 지금은 한국에 둘, 이곳에 네 형제가 살고 있지만, 이민 첫 개척자로의 애환 속에 갈등하며 때로는 어려움을 이기지 못해 마음고생하며 외로워 울던 그 시절의 애틋한 옛 추억과 함께 흥겨운 리듬을 타고 '두만강 푸른물에…' '황성옛터….' '옛 시인의 노래' '무인도' ' 개똥벌레' 등등 쉬지 않고 가라오케 반주에 맞춰 이어지는 노래와 웃음소리와 정겨운 대화가 줄줄이 흐르는 속에 아득한 옛 추억 속으로 데려다 준다.

어린 시절 친정아버지께서 약주를 드시면 기분 좋아 부르시던 옛날가요를 들으며 성장기를 보낸 덕택인가. 언제나 풍부한 성량의 목소리의 주인공이셨던 아버지의 유전형질의 목소리를 모두가 물려 받았나, 우리 형제들의 노래 실력은 제법 들을만하고 나무랄 데 없는 목소리들을 가진 걸 보면 말이다. 유난히 오늘은 30여 년 전 고국나들이에서의 추억도 잊을 수 없다. 투병 중이셨던 어머니를 위로하며 동생과 교회에서 듀엣으로 특송(어머니의 사랑보다 더 한 것이 있으랴) 을 부른 적이 있었다. 딸들의 찬양을 들으시며 교회 앞좌석에 힘들게 앉아 미소지으시던 어머니의 초췌한 모습이 떠오르니 핑 도는 눈물을 주체하기 힘들다.

형제들이란 어린 시절엔 한 이불에서 함께 자며 어울려 놀던 아름다운 과거가 있기 마련이고 현재와 미래를 소유하며 살아가야하는 필연적인 혈연의 관계가 아닌가. 그러나 형제간에도 사랑을 나눠주는 법과 사랑을 받아들이는 법을 배우는 것이 인생에서 가장 중요한 것이라 생각한다. 이민의 삶이 지치고 힘들었어도 열심히 일하면서 긍정적인 마음을 갖고 서로서로 격려하며 사랑함과 건강함속에서 오늘의 여유로운 삶을 살아가는 형제들이 있어 한없이 고맙고 흐뭇한 마음이다.

부지런히 살아가는 즐거움처럼 여유 있는 인생은 없다고 생각한다. 먼 옛일들을 떠올리면 그것은 언제나 하나의 꽃으로 피어오르듯이 삶을 되돌아보는 이력의 세계는 언제나 잡다한 아름다움뿐이다. 그것은 하나님이 나를 선택해주신 은혜요, 나에게는 끝없는기쁨이다. 한없는 감사가 넘쳐난다.

한 겨울 고장 난 히터

어느덧 겨울의 한복판에 와 있다.

아침부터 뿌옇게 흐린 하늘이더니 갑자기 세찬 바람과 함께 하얀 눈발을 뿌리기 시작한다. 잠시 주춤하고는 또 다시 폭설로 변해 한참을 더 뿌려대고는 뚝 그쳤다

순식간에 차에 얹어진 눈을 치우느라 땀을 흠뻑 흘리고. 큰길의 눈들은 어디로 날아갔는지 난 스파로 달려갔다. 운동도 부지런해야 한다고 부지런을 떨면서 열심히 몸을 움직이며 하루를 시작한다. 실은 은퇴 후 하루종일 남편과 함께 하는 시간 속에 서로의 취미생활을 적절히 이용한다는 것이 쉽지가 않지만 서로를 방해하지 않는 범위 내에서 즐긴다.

황혼이 지고 뿌연 밤이 깔리기 시작하는 걸 보면 겨울 해가 정말 짧다. 계절이 변화(사계절)를 일으키듯 우리들의 삶 또한 많은 변화를 일으킨다

고 생각한다. 세월의 힘은 속이지 못해 얼굴엔 잔주름이 늘어가고 가능한 외적인 면에 무관하게 편안한 삶을 즐기려고 노력하지만 때로는 어려움이 슬그머니 내 곁에 찾아와 힘들게 하기도 한다. 그러나 철저히 아침에 살아 있음에 기쁨을 느끼며, 저녁에 이불속에 들어감에 감사하며, 지내는 일상이 행복함이요 축복이 아닌가.

오늘 아침에 자리에서 일어나 보니 방안의 공기가 썰렁하니 냉기가 확 돈다. 깜짝 놀라 지하실로 내려간 남편은 히터가 고장 났다고 서두르고, 난 불현듯 떠오르는 그 옛날의 추억 속으로 빠져든다. 꺼진 연탄에 불붙여 놓고 냉방에서 떨며 불이 피기까지 기다리다가 방 한쪽 따스한 온기가 전해져오면 마음마저 훈훈해지던 그 때가 언제였던가. 연탄은 활활 타지만 웃풍이 센 방에서 자던 어린시절의 아릿한 추억과 추운 겨울 밤 화롯불에 손을 호호 불면서 고구마랑 밤을 구워주시며 옛날 얘기를 들려주시던 어머니가 마냥 그리워진다. 요즈음은 오븐에 고구마를 구워 먹을 때면 모락모락 올라오는 김과 함께 어머니의 목소리가 아른거려 안경에 서리는 김 뒤에는 눈시울에 흐르는 눈물이 있다.

향이 가득한 커피를 타서 마시니 그 따뜻함이 손길을 타고 오르며 마음은 어느 사이 발랄한 생동감으로 꿈틀거린다. 고장 났던 히터는 기술자의 도움으로 방안 가득 더운 공기를 뿜어대기 시작한다. 우리의 삶에도 한 겨울에 히터가 고장 난 것 같이 하나의 가치에 열심히 매달려 있다가 잘 풀리지 않을 때 우울함 속에서 한참을 허우적대며 방황하는 마음의 온기가 꺼지는 날이 있을지 모른다. 그래도 우리는 무던히 마음을 다스려 다시 불을 피워 올려야 하는 노력의 날들이기를 바란다. 순간 어느 책에서 읽은 구절이 생각난다. "마음은 자신의 가장 소중한 재산이다. 생각은 우물을 파는 것과 닮았다고 한다. 처음에는 흐려져 있지만 차차 맑아지고 있음을…"

날씨가 추울 때는 따뜻한 불이 그립듯 마음이 추울 때는 따뜻한 인정 또한 그리워지는 것. 마음의 추위는 어떻게 해서든 달래져야만 한다. 배고픔에 장사가 없듯 추위에도 장사가 없지 않은가. 이 세상의 모든 사람들이 따뜻한 온기를 조금만 세상에 나누어준다면 이 세상은 조금 더 따뜻한 세상이 될 것이라 믿는다.

희망 가득한 계절에

어느 새 노란 개나리, 수선화가 활짝, 갖가지 꽃들이 봄의 정취를 마음껏 뽐내며 경쟁하듯 피워내는 희망 가득한 계절이 돌아왔다. 얼마 전만해도 온 천지는 흰눈이 덮히고 햇빛을 받은 들판은 보석가루처럼 반짝여 눈이부셨다. 주위에 늘어선 나무들은 우중충한 푸른 가지 위에 흰 눈을 얹고 힘겹게 축 늘어져, 햇볕에 녹은 눈(雪)물을 한 방울씩 떨구고 있다. 바람이 불 때마다 눈가루가 하얗게 날려 와 내 뺨을 스치고 지나갈 때마다 낭만이 물씬 풍겨주었는데, 웬지 오늘은 함박눈이 펑펑 쏟아지던 아득한 이민 초기의 옛 추억속으로 빠져든다.

갓 배운 운전이 마냥 서툴러 가파른 언덕을 오르지 못 해 쩔쩔매고 미끄러지고 벌벌 떨고, 남편의 대리운전으로 언덕을 올라 직장을 다니던 그 어려웠던 시절이 엊그제 같은데. 어느덧 30여년의 세월이 흘러 은퇴한 나이가 됐으니 말이다. 우린 추위가 엄습해오는 한겨울엔 좀 따뜻한 남쪽으로 휴가를 떠나곤 한다. 평상시엔 말이 없는 남편이지만 장거리 여행 때는 항상 대화의 광장 문을 활짝 열어주어 가슴속에 쌓였던 우울한 노폐물까지도 확 씻어 내주는 기회를 갖게 되니 얼마나 좋은지. 대화란 공감할 수 있다면 분명히 신진대사가 될 수 있는게 아닌가.

노스캐롤라이나를 이어 사우스캐롤라이나를 지나치는 길목엔 유난히도 울창한 소나무들이 즐비, 싱싱한 푸르른 솔가지사이로 불어오는 바람 속에 향긋한 솔냄새가 물씬 실려있는 것 같다. 은퇴를 하고 추위를 피해 따뜻한 남쪽에 와 2~3개월 동안 콘도를 렌트해 골프를 치며 한가로운 삶을 즐기다 간다는 철새같은 은퇴한 부부들과의 만남. 그들도 지금은 희망 가득한 봄의 내음에 취해 삶의 기쁨을 누리고 있으리라.

흐르는 세월 속에 기억도 흘러간다. 때로는 남편과 의견대립으로 냉전의 깊은 골이 생겨 멀리 떠나고 싶은 마음이 생긴적도 있었고, 마냥 섭섭해 나 혼자 베개를 적신 적도 있었으나 세월도 기쁨도 슬픔도 구름처럼 지나가는 인생의 무상함을 느끼는 나이가 되고 보니 한평생을 함께한 그이, 언제나 가정 중심의 부지런함과 성실함에 고마움과 감사를 새삼 느끼게 되니 뒤늦게 철이 들어가는가 보다.

희망 가득한 계절은 왔는데 이민의 희로애락을 함께하며, 기쁨을 배로 느끼며, 슬픔을 반으로 나누며, 형제같이 지냈던 지인들의 별세소식들이 가슴을 아프게 한다. 생명을 주신자도, 취하시는자도 하나님이시니 이제는 이세상의 모든 고통과 멍에에서 벗어나 오직 주님의 품안에서 고이 잠드시길 기도드리며 위로 해본다.

세상것에 매달리지말고 영원한것은 없다는 진리를 깨달으며 죽음이란 대책없이 쉽게 우리를 찾아온다는 것을 알았고, 나 역시 언제 찾아올줄 모르는 죽음앞에서 인생이 산다는 것이 허무함을 느껴지기도 한다. 저세상으로 돌아갈 때는 빈손인 것을, 결국 중요한 것은 우리가 얼마나 힘차게 자기를 꾸준히 건설했는가 하는 것이 아니겠는가.

봄의 정취가 흠뻑 쏟아지는 좋은 계절! 봄은 정녕 기쁨에 싸인 계절이며 생명이 약동하는 계절이다. 연한 연두색으로 휘이휘이 나무가지마다 감싸듯 추욱 늘어져가는 수양버들을 바라보며 점점 녹색의 진함이 묻어나는 희망 가득한 계절을 맞아 더 멋진 삶의 푸르른 일상으로 펼쳐보리라.

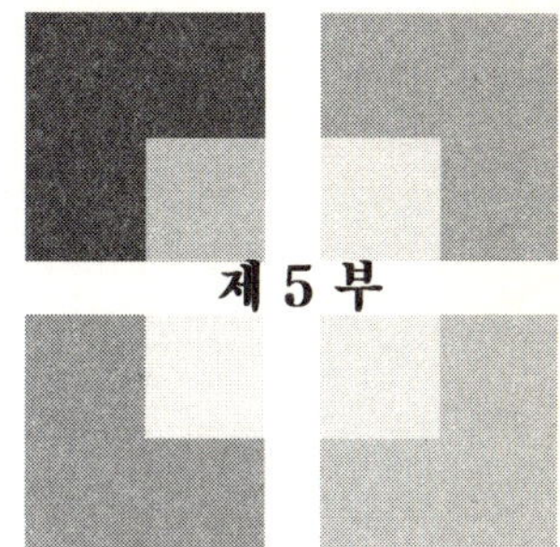

제5부

뜨루히요(Trujillo)의 풍경

간밤에 천지를 뒤흔들 듯 '쾅 쾅' 소리치며 번개가 번쩍이고, 엄청난 빗줄기가 온 지붕을 내리치더니 오늘 아침은 시치미를 뚝떼고 맑은 하늘에 흰 구름이 두둥실, 나뭇가지에 매달린 무성한 잎사귀는 불어오는 실바람에 맞추어 가늘게 춤을 추고 있다. 눈부신 밝은 햇살은 흠뻑 젖은 대지를 말리느라 습한 더운 김을 뿜어대며 86도가 훨씬 넘는 사우나를 만들어 놓는 중이다. 잠깐 밖을 나갔다 왔는데 땀에 범벅이 되어 시원한 에어컨에 감사가 절로난다.

난 요즈음 얼마 전 다녀온 페루에서 열흘간의 생활이 눈앞에 아른거리며 추억을 더듬는 버릇을 숨기지 못한다. 뜨루히요는 페루의 수도 리마(Lima)에서 북쪽으로 500 마일 떨어진 3대 도시로 계절적으로는 6월이 겨울철이라고는 하나 얇은 스웨터를 걸칠 정도의 기후다. 아침마다 뿌옇게 흐린 날씨에 안개비가 내리며 촉촉이 젖은 도로변을 걷는 재킷을 입은 사람들의 물결이 홍수를 이룬다.

노란 택시들의 행렬, 오토바이를 개조해 옛날 우리나라 인력거 비슷한 울긋불긋 포장을 친 '모타 탁씨'(현지인 들이 그렇게 부른다) 들. 길가에 늘어선 행상들의 초라한 모습들, 군데군데 모여 정부에 항의하는 데모대들의 아우성은 가난에 못 이긴 국민들의 몸부림일 것이다.

하루는 우리가 탄 차 앞에 만원버스가 덜커덕거리며 달려간다.

아, 이게 웬 일이야, 차 뒤창에 엄연히 '신촌' '이대 앞' 이라는 한글로 쓴 선명하고도 큰 글씨가 눈에 들어온다. 한국에서 중고차를 수입해와 외국 차라는 것을 자랑삼아 지워버리지 않고 그냥 운행한다는 거다. 어떤 버스는 '미아리' '영등포' '수유리' ,녹번동' ,'노량진'을 달고 달린다.

노란 택시는 주로 한국에서 들어온 조그마한 티코다.

하루 10솔(1달라=3.5솔)이면 4가족이 살 수 있다는데 그 돈을 벌 곳이 없어 길거리에 나와 서성대는 젊은 남자들. 집은 흙모래로 다닥다닥 연립주택같고 지붕는 납짝하게 함석으로 씌워져 있으며 흙모래 바닥에 판자를 깔아 침실로 쓰고 한켠은 부엌으로 물까지 사서 써야하니 파리가 왕왕댄다.

이른 새벽 수산 시장의 풍경은 질퍽질퍽 비린내가 물씬 풍기는 갖가지 종류의 크고 작은 이름 모를 생선들, 특히나 타월만한 크기의 오징어, 문어, 1m 가 훨씬 넘는 상어가 눈길을 끌었으며, 뜨루히요의 큰시장엔 산더미 같이 쌓인 바나나와 500여 종류나 된다는 감자와 고구마의 전시장 같고 알맹이가 엄지 손가락만한 찰옥수수, 사탕수수, 갖가지 종류의 과일, 콩, 쌀, 붉은 고추, 파란 고추 등이 풍성한 이색적인 시장이다.

조그만 아이들이 짐 실어준다고 세 발 구루마를 끌고 졸졸 따라다닌다. 뜨루히요의 사람들은 어쩜 그렇게도 이목구비가 반듯하고 큼직큼직하면서도 매력적으로 생겼는지 페루에는 성형외과가 없다는 말같이 모두가 미남 미녀들이다. 인사할 때는 남녀 구별 없이 껴안고 볼에 뽀뽀하며, 감사를 표시 할때는 더 꼭 껴안고 'Muchas gracias' 하며 볼에 침이 튈 정도로 정열적으로 인사한다.

대낮에도 강도와 소매치기가 들끓어 좀 산다는 집은 쥐꼬리만한 돈을 주고 24시간 경비원을 고용한 집도 있다. 3모작하는 기후 조건이 좋은 환경에서 보다 나은 삶을 위해서 발버둥치는 모습을 보면서 강도와 소매치기가 판치지 않는 바르게 사는 사람과 노력해서 거둬지는 결실의 기쁨을 갖는 사람이 많아질 때 뜨루히요의 풍경은 보다 아름다워 질 것이란 생각을 한다.

러시아와 북유럽 여행기

3개월 전부터 계획했던 러시아와 북유럽 여행일이 다가왔다.

어쩌면 Lucky seven이 줄줄이(7월7일2007년) 세개가 들어 있는 날이고 보니 분명 행운을 안고 다닐것 같은 날, 오후 5시 30분 워싱턴 덜레스공항을 이륙, 코펜하겐을 경유, 다음 날 오후 3시 모스크바 국제공항에 도착했다.

공항을 벗어나는 대로(大路)엔 신축 고층건물들의 공사가 한창, 러시아의 경제발전이 보이는듯, 광활한 국토의 30%는 녹지화로, 도시의 건물은 50여년이 넘은 고풍스럽고 견고한 예술품과 같았다. 지하철, 버스, 전차의 운행속에 많은 인파가 바쁘게 움직이고 바로 코앞에 움직이는 전차는 정크장에나 갈만한 녹이 많이 난 35여년의 역사를 지녔다는 앤틱 같은 전차가 운행함에 놀랐다.

길목마다 꽃가게가 많고, 꽃으로 단장한 잔디밭과 이층, 삼층 꽃바구니를 세워놓아 어찌나 아름답고 화려하든지. 러시아인(人)들이 아름다움을 유난히 좋아한다는 민족성을 보는것 같았지만, 미소없는 러시아인들의 표정은 무겁기까지해 아직도 사회주의의 사상이 몸에 배인것 같았다.

후덕지근한 날씨에, 높은 빌딩 창문마다 매미 같은 에어컨통이 아슬아슬하게 매달려있다. 늦은시간 서커스를 관람후, 호텔에 투숙. 다음날 아침 러시아의 상징 붉은광장(아름답고, 이쁘고, 좋다는 뜻)으로 갔다. 광장안 서남쪽에 위치한 성 바실리성당은 여덟개의 양파머리처럼 생긴 지붕으로 독특한 양식을 갖추고 있어 얼마나 아름답든지. 바로 오른편에는 크레믈린 궁전이 엄숙하게, 그 옆에 유명한 '레닌의 묘' 가 자리해있고, 뒷편으로 돌면 푸친대통령의 집무실이 있는 환한색 노란건물이 서 있다.

붐비는 관광객들은 기념 촬영하느라 연신 셔터를 눌러대고. 249년의 역사를 지닌 세계적인 명문 모스크바 국립대학은 도시 가운데 우뚝 서 사면이 똑같은 양식의 하얀 벽돌로 견고하게 지어진 이 대학에서 6명의 노벨상 수상자가 배출됐다. 이어 노보데비치묘지에 안장된 엘친과 후르스쵸프의 묘소를 들러보고, 러시아의 태양, 신 러시아 문학의 창시자로 불리었던 '푸시킨'이 다녔던 학교인 푸시킨박물관을 관람했다. 푸시킨의 동상앞에서 그의 유명한 시(詩) '생활이 그대를 속일지라도…'를 읊으며 낭만에 젖어보았다. 톨스토이(「죄와 벌」의 작가)의 동상이 저만치 서 있다. 좁은 길목이긴해도 카페와 상점이 줄비한 낭만적인 아르바트 거리에선 바이올린 연주가들이 한국인을 알아 보고 애국가를 연주해 감격하기도했다.

칠흙같은 어둠이 깔릴 깊은 밤12시 인데도 대낮같은 백야의 도시에서 1200개의 객실을 갖춘 묵직한 호텔에서 묵고, 다음 날 아침 일정에 따라 모스크바를 뒤로하고 세인 피터스버그를 향해 비행기로 2시간만에 레닌그라드에 도착했다. 강과 운하가 곳곳에 펼쳐져 북유럽의 베니스라는 말이 실감나는 도시. 시가지를 감돌며 흐르는 네바강을 끼고 낭만과 예술이 함께 숨쉬는 에르미타쥐 박물관(비밀의 방)엔 1,000개가 넘는 전시실에 약 250만점이 전시되어 있으며 특히 화가 고호의「언덕 위에 집」이 눈에 들어 한참을 서있기도 했다.

피터대제의 여름궁전과 분수공원, 카잔성당, 황금빛 거대한 둥근지붕을 갖춘 높이 101m의 세계제일의 멋진 성당인 이삭성당 등 수많은 유적들을 둘러보았다.

성 바실리 성당(러시아 모스크바에서)

한 극장에서 유명한 발레「백조의 호수」를 관람하고, 선물가게마다 나무로 만든 인형속에 또 인형이 들어있는 '마뜨루시카(엄마)인형'이 주를 이루고, 갖가지 꽃들과 푸른 잔디, 강변의 건물들이 어울려 환상적인 도시의 분위기가 넘쳐나는 세인 피터스버그에서 3일간을 머물렀지만 많은 미련이 남는데, 일정에 따라 핀란드의 수도 헬싱키를 향해 기차를 타고 빠르게 지나치는 차창 밖 이국의 경관을 놓칠세라 감상하기에 바빴다.

세인 피터스버그에서 기차를 타고 2시간만에 핀란드국경에 도착, 입국통관하고, 4시간을 더 달려 핀란드의 수도 헬싱키역에 도착했다. 해가 서산으로 기우는 시간속에 때아닌 하늘에 곱게 펼쳐진 이국의 무지개를 보고 감탄하면서 항구가 훤히 보이는 한 호텔에서 짐을 풀었다. 핀란드는 총인구 약 516만명으로 면적은 남한의 3배, 유럽에서 다섯번째로 큰나라로써 국토의 70%가 산림과 호수(18만 7,888개)와 바위로 이루어진 천혜의 자연경관을 살려 마음껏 누릴 수 있는 관광의 낙원이다.

조선업이 발달해 우리나라에 금강산유람선을 수출. 사회보장제도가 잘된나라로서 특징은 양성 평등으로 현재 대통령도 여성, 각 분야에서 여성이 차지하는 비중은 50%가 넘는 여성권리가 막강한 나라다. 북유럽에서 유일한 공화국으로 독자적인 언어를 사용하고 멕시코만류와 발트 해의 영향으로 온화한 편이다.

다음날 아침 버스로 이동중 시벨리우스공원에 도착, 핀란드의 유명한 작곡가인 시벨리우스의 얼굴동상과 파이프상을 둘러보았다. 이 파이프상은 바람이 불면 아름다운 음률을 낸다는 멋진 작품이다. 많은 층계위에 우뚝 선 헬싱키 대성당(원로원 광장)안을 올라가 보고, 성당앞 광장에서 펼친 장엄한 군악대 사열을 지켜보는 행운도 가졌다. 러시아황제 알렉산드르 2세의 웅장한 동상에 올라가 디카에 추억을 담느라고 법석을 떨기도 했다. 암반을 뚫어서 만든 템펠리아우키오(1969년 완성))교회는 바위속이라 음향효과가 뛰어나다고 했으나 시간이 맞지않아 조용히 들러보는데 만족해야만했다.

갖가지 먹거리를 파는 마켓 카우파토리광장과 작은배들이 닿는 부두, 유람선이 오고 가는 항구 바로 건너편에 시청과 대통령궁이 있어 놀랐다. 분명 권력을 남용하지 않는 서민과의 평등의 나라임을 보는것 같았다.

멀지않은 곳에 핀란드와 스웨덴을 잇는 5만 8천톤급의 호화유람선 실자라인(silja line=바다표범)터미날에 도착, 탑승 승객 3,000명을 실은 초호화 유람선은 헬싱키에서 스톡홀롬으로 가는 발트 해안에는 약 2만여개의 아름다운 섬들이 줄지어 있고, 파란하늘에 떠있는 뭉게구름, 푸른 숲속에 숨은듯이 띄엄띄엄 들어서 있는 집들은 코발트색의 바다와 조화를 이루어 채색의 풍경화를 펼쳐놓은것 같았고. 아름다운 협만을 계속해서 빠져나가는 실자는 이름에 걸맞게 한여름 밤의 심포니라도 울릴듯 뱃고동소리를 울리며 바이킹들이 활보했던 역사의 대양를 질주하는데 이곳을 두고 북유럽여행의 절정으로 꼽는다.

세차게 부는 바람을 맞으며 갑판에 나가서서 백야의 아름다움이 드리워진 발틱해의 일몰과 일출을 보겠다고 잔뜩 벌렸는데 그만 시간을 못마춰 못내 아쉬움을 남기고,. 밤을 밝히며 한 밤을 바다에서 16시간동안 항해, 아침 9시에 스웨덴의 수도 스톡(통나무)홀롬(섬)항에 도착했다. 승객 3,000여명이 빠져나가느라 북새통을 이루고 대기한 버스를 타고, 길목에 즐비한 자작나무의 싱그러움속에 도시 전체가 예술품처럼 정교해 건축박물관이라해도 과언이 아니다. 핀란드와 마찬가지로 건축물을 새로 짓는 것은 법으로 엄격히 규제한단다.

면적은 450,000평방km로 한반도의 약 2배, 유로화는 사용하지않고 별도의 화폐 스웨덴 '크로나'를 사용한다. 노벨상의 원조자 노벨은 아이러니하게도 다이나마이트를 발명한 사람으로 스톡홀름이 고향이다. 문학상은 스톡홀름 (한림원)에서 시상한다. 14개의 섬이 모여서 만들어진 도시지만 다리만 750개의 넓은 수면과 운하때문에 북극의 베네치아로 불리우는 스톡홀름에서 1박 2일의 짧은 일정을 마치고, 다음 일정지 노르웨이의 수도 오슬로로 가기 위해, 멋진 요트로 꽉메운 멜라린호수가를 벗어나며 공항으로 달려갔다.

노벨 평화상 시상식이 열리는 도시, 노르웨이의 수도 오슬로에 도착했다. 호텔에 짐을 놓고, 아까운 시간을 놓칠세라 우산을 들고 거리로 나섰다. 온통 비에 젖어버린 오슬로 중심가를 걸어보는 토요일 저녁, 젊은 남녀들로 꽉메운 상가들, 즐비한 상품에 기웃거리며 낭만에 흠뻑 젖는 첫밤을 맞았다.

북유럽의 스칸디나비아반도의 서쪽에 위치해 봄, 가을이 짧긴하지만 유일하게도 사계절이 있고, 250만년전에 시작된 1,700여곳의 빙하가 녹아 호

모노리스 조각공원(노르웨이)

르는 호수가 전 국토에 널려있는 호수와 빙하로 이루어진 나라다. 대체적으로 따뜻한 것은 맥시코 만류 덕택이란다. 북부 노르웨이는 백야(白夜)의 지방으로 5월~7월은 해가 지지않고, 11월~1월까지는 해가 지평선위로 떠오르지 않는단다. 1969년부터 석유가 터져 세계인이 부러워하는 축복의 땅으로 교육은 대학교까지 국가가 지원해주는 나라다.

다음날 아침 오슬로를 출발, 5시간만에 동계올림픽(홀멘콜른스키 점프대)이 두번이나 열렸던 릴리함메르에 도착했다. 저켠에 펼쳐있는 호반의 풍은 계곡의 여왕이라 부를 만큼 경관이 아름답고 얼마나 수려한 곳인지 감탄사를 연발했다. 아름답고 웅장한 협곡을 따라 버스로 이동, 만년설이 뒤덮인 산과 금잔디를 입혀놓은것 같은 마을, 해발 600m의 산장호텔에서 낭만적인 밤을 보냈다.

다음날 아침 꾸불꾸불 아슬아슬한 계곡을 넘는데 위험천만한 절벽위에 겁없이 앉아있는 양떼들, 먹을 것을 찾아 관광객의 손길을 기다리며 길가에 진을치고 앉아있는 소떼들. 디카에 순간의 모습을 담느라 몸살을 냈다. 정말 말로는 설명할 수 없는 자연의 경이로움에 그저 멍해질 노르웨이 여행의 하이라이트로 꼽히는 게이랑게르에 도착했다.

270m에 달하는 거대한 폭포가 푸른 바다처럼 피요르드로 쏟아져내려 강을 이루고 있었다. 피요르드는 약 100만년전 이 지역을 덮고 있던 빙하가 그 무게를 감당하지 못하고 내려앉으면서 땅을 밀어내 U자 형태의 계곡을 만들어 바닷물이 스며들어 만들어진 곳이다. 훼리를 타고, 피요르드

를 감상하며 2시간가량을 지나는동안 곳곳에 우뚝선 기암절벽과 수많은 폭포의 신비스러운 비경이 그림엽서같고, 브닉스달 빙하로 가는 길목엔 높은 산들이 첩첩이 솟아있어 록키산맥이나 알프스를 연상케한다.

빙하의 대륙을 보기위해 묵직한 짚차를 타고 계곡을 올라 북유럽의 최대의 빙하를 만났다. 수십만년전부터 내린 눈이 쌓이고 형성된 빙하의 빛깔은 푸른기운이 감도는 흰색에 가깝다. 허지만 지구의 온난화현상으로 빙하가 점차 녹아 줄어들고 있다는 사실이 무척 아쉬움으로 남는다. 오슬로의 바이킹 박물관을 관람하고, 칼요한의 거리를 걸어보고, 비겔란드 조각공원으로 갔다.

10만평의 공원, 입구부터 중앙에 이르기까지 인간의 탄생과 죽음에 관련된 조각품들이 펼쳐져 있고, 197개의 작품중, 특이한것은 모노리스(하나로된 돌기둥) 조각품은 인간의 본질적인 문제인 사랑, 증오, 질투, 질병등을 테마로해서 완성된 작품으로 오슬로의 최고의 명물이다.

작곡가 에드워드 그닉(Edward Grieg)의 집을 방문, 더욱이 「솔베이지의 노래」를 작곡했던 오두막집엔 그의 유물이 그대로 전시돼 있고, 가까운곳에 그의 부부 납골당이 있다. '주 하나님 지으신 모든 세계…..' 그리고 '아 목동아…'가 절로 흥얼거려지는 노르웨이의 아름다운 순수한 자연경관은 평생을 잊지못할 멋진 추억을 간직케 했다.

노르웨이의 수도 오슬로공항을 이륙, 1시간 반만에 서부 유럽의 중앙에서 북쪽 반도에 자리잡고 있는 덴마크의 수도 코펜하겐에 도착했다. 스칸디나비아 반도와 유럽대륙을 연결하는 관문의 도시로 깔끔하게 정돈된 거리와 곳곳의 공원 그리고 대형 여객선과 요트로 늘어선 운하에서 북유럽 특유의 여유와 낭만을 느낄 수 있었다.

덴마크의 공식이름은 덴마크 왕국. 1972년에 왕좌에 오른 마르그레데 2

세여왕이 통치하고 있는 군주국이다. 아말리엔 보르궁전은 소박한 저택같은 분위기다. 여왕이 궁전에 머무르는 날에만 왕궁지붕에 깃발이 꽂힌단다. 더욱이 공식행사가 아니면 보디가이드 없이 혼자다니는 극히 자유로운 분위기가 넘치는 나라라니 더욱 정이 간다. 낙농의 나라. 바다에 심은 풍차로 풍력발전소가 발달해 많은 외화를 벌어들이는 나라. 인슐린 생산국이며. GNP 5만불로 세계 1위로 행복지수가 높은 나라로 사회보장제도가 잘되어 있는 복지국가다.

겨울이 길고 엄청 추워 루마치스환자와 우울증환자가 계속 늘고 있어 고민도 따르는 나라라니, 춘하추동이 있는 미국 워싱턴에 산다는 것이 얼마나 행복인가 감사가 절로난다. 길가에 빽빽이 서 있는 자전거와 줄지어 타고다니는 자전거 천국. 국민 일인당 한대로, 자전거와 수영을 못하면 덴마크사람이 아니란다. 달리는 자전거는 멈추지 않는다는 「원더풀 코펜하겐」 이란 유행한 노래도 있다.

도시의 중심인 시청사 건물 입구에는 코펜하겐의 창립자인 압상론동상이 근엄하게 무게를 잡고 서 있고, 덴마크가 자랑하는 실존주의 철학자 '쉬렌 키에르케고르'(죽음에 이르는 병)의 동상도 서 있어 둘러보았다. 이 도시의 집들은 말그대로 동화책 배경그림에 나오는 그림속에 담긴것같이 얼마나 아름다운지. 청동오리와 백조가 유유히 떠다니는 프레데릭보르성은 (백조의 성)은 너무나도 아름답고, 공원은 한폭의 그림을 펼쳐놓은 것 같다. 언덕위에 자리한 거대한 분수 '게피온의 샘'은 마차를 몰고 질주하는 거대한 소의 입에서 쏟아내는 분수인데 가히 장관을 이루고 있다.

한스 크리스티안 안데르센(1805~1875년)의 삶에서 「미운 오리새끼」 「인어공주」 「성냥팔이 소녀」 와 같은 수많은 걸작으로 세계 어린이들의 마음에 지울 수 없는 인상을 남긴 아동문학의 거장이 한때 기거했던 붉은벽돌의 한 아파트를 가까이서 바라보기도 했다. 바다내음이 물씬풍기는 해변에는 안데르센의 동화 인어공주에서 따와, 1913년 에드바르트 에릭슨이 조각한 인어공주상이 북적대는 관광객으로 둘러쌓인 바닷가 암초위에 안데르센의 소설을 타고 그 유명세를 톡톡히 치루고 있었다. 인간세계로도 고향인 바다로도 돌아갈 수 없는 반인 반어인 공주의 자태는 그녀의 신세만큼 처연해 보이는 반면 상상외로 그리 크지않은 작으마한 몸매로 처량하게 바위에 걸터 앉아, 고개를 숙인 모습속에서 애처러움과 안타까움과 슬픔을 한껏 뿜어내고 있어 보는사람으로 하여금 진한 감정의 추억을 갖게 한다.

여행이란 지금까지 숨가쁘게 앞만보고 달려온 현대인들에게 자기자신을 되집어 볼 수 있는 참된 순간속에서 자신의 인생을 반추하는 과정이기도 하고 또한 인생의 어느 한순간을 빠르지않게 천천히 걷고자하는 이들의 한 쉼터가 아닐까. 12박 13일동안 긴 여행에서 돌아가 쉴 수 있는 내집이 있음에 더욱 감사함과 탈없이 행복한 여행길을 지켜주신 하나님의 무한한 사랑에 감사드린다.

마이애미의 풍경과 헤밍웨이의 집

마이애미의 밤은 하늘거리는 야자수가 숨쉬면서 내뿜는 향긋함과 바다 내음이 풍기는 비릿한 자연의 냄새와 그리고 휘황찬란한 가로등의 불빛이 또다른 느낌을 주고 있었다.

친구 부부의 마중을 받으며 공항을 벗어나자 두툼한 자켓을 벗었다. 질주하는 차창밖 더운 공기속의 밤은 점점 깊어가고 별빛은 더욱더 밝고 청명하게 바다위로 쏟아지고 있었다.

친구와의 정(友情) 이란 정을 나눠주는 법과 정을 받아들이는 법을 배우며 정답게 이어가는 것이며, 우리인생의 길동무가 얼마나 삶에 기쁨이 되는지. 마이애미 친구 부부는 30여년간 성실과 친절을 모토로 사업을 하면서 크게 성공하여 얼마전 은퇴후 마이애미 고급동네에 멋진 콘도를 second home으로 마련해 철새같이 뉴욕에서, 마이애미에서 일년을 반으로 갈라 낭만적인 삶을 즐기고 있다.

미네소타, 뉴욕, 워싱톤의 동창 친구 부부들을 초대해서 세밀하게 계획한 스케줄에 맞추어 펼쳐지는 하루하루가 시작되었다. 습한 바람부는 아침 풀잎은 젖었고 하늘은 우유빛이었다. 골프장 한켠 연못의 물이 찰랑거리는 소리가 들리고, 유난히 긴 부리와 핑크빛 다리를 가진 하얀 거위들이 털을 흔드는 소리도 들렸다. 뿐만이 아니었다. 엄마거북이와 아기거북이가 헤엄치다 말고 마주보는척하다 별안간 입맞춤하고는 좋아라 어쩔줄몰라 몸부림치는 귀여운 모습을 놓치지 않고 볼 수 있는 행운도 가질 수 있었고, 자그마한 악어들이 느긋하게 기어다니는 것을 보며 우린 흥분해서 마냥 그 자리에 서 있었다.

누런 열매가 탐스럽게 달려있는 야자수 숲과 호수의 기막힌 조화, 그 속에서 에메랄드빛과 짙은초록으로 비쳐진 물살을 가르는 모터소리에 맞추어 흰거품과 물방울을 마구 뿌려대며 바다로 달려나가는 보트에 실려 꿈같은 환상에 젖어 우린 약속이나 한듯 '싼타루치아'를 목청껏 소리내어 불러댔다. 태양빛이 작열하는 가운데 부서질듯 맑은공기, 마이애미 시에서 서남쪽으로 130마일 떨어진 Key West를 향해 뻥뚫린 고속도로와 길게 길게 늘어진 도로, 7마일이나 되는 긴다리를 달려가는 차창에 스치는 경치는 한폭의 그림의 연속이었다.

8인승 밴에 몸들을 꽉 채우고 동요로 시작해서 팝송과 트로트까지 네 커플이 쏟아 내는 멜로디와 얘기들은 모두가 타임머신을 타고 40여년 전 시간 속에 들어가 있는듯한 착각 속에 수많은 아름다운 추억을 수놓았다.

마침내 우린 KeyWest에 자리 잡고 있는 어네스트 헤밍웨이의 집에 도착했다. 잘 정리된 정원과 실외 수영장을 갖춘 이층집으로, 그의 애완동물이었던 여섯개의 발가락을 가진 수많은 고양이 후예들의 재롱이 관광객의 시선을 끈다.

이 집은 1851해양 건축가이자 난파선 구조원인 에이사 티프트라는 사람에 의해 지어졌고 1931년 헤밍웨이의 소유가 되었다. 1961년 헤밍웨이 사망 이후, 사업가 버니스 딕슨 여사가 매입 해 1968년에 국가 유적으로 채택되어 오늘날까지 Mrs Dickson 가족의 재산으로 남아있다.

그는 61년 간의 생애동안 멋진 삶을 즐겼으며, 소설분야에서 퓰리처상을 수상했고 문학부문에서 노벨상을 타기도 했다. 그의 작업장은 그가 사용했던 그대로 보존되어 있으며 그가 아끼던 타자기, 그가 모아오던 기념품들과 서적들이 모두 그대로 있다. 그 작업실에서 그는 「오후에 죽음」 「아프리카의 푸른언덕」 「가진자와 못가진자」 「누구를 위하여 종을 울리나」 「킬리만자로의 눈」 등 수많은 단편소설을 썼다. 이어 가까운 곳에 있는 '90마일 쿠바 위령탑'을 가보았다.

키 웨스트에서 바다를 경계로 90마일 거리밖에 안 되는 쿠바에서 미국으로 헤엄쳐 밀항하다 목숨을 잃은 수많은 쿠바인을 추모하며 세워진 위령탑을 보면서 숙연해지기도 했다.

현실을 벗어나 아름다운 정취에 빠져보는 시간이 얼마나 값있는 시간인지. 여행이란 자연속에서 내 삶을 음미해보고 새로운 에너지를 얻어 돌아오는 것이 아닐까. 언젠가는 가보리라 싶었던 어네스트 헤밍웨이의 집을 방문하도록 시작에서 끝나는 날까지 최선의 것만을 계획한 친구부부에게 잊을 수 없는 추억을 안겨준 감사의 뜨거움을 전하고 싶다.

브라질 리오에서 남미의 파리까지

성큼 여름이 찾아왔나 착각할 만큼 한낮의 더위가 어리둥절했던 지난달 3월 초 한 여름의 나라로 여행을 떠났다. 두툼한 재킷을 걸치는 짐스러움도 없이 저녁시간에 내셔널 공항을 떠나 마이아미를 거쳐 장장 10시간 넘게 밤을 밝히며 날아 다음날 아침 8시경 브라질 제2의 도시인 리오 데 자네이로에 도착했다.

인구 약 1,000만 명, 보사노바(세월의 흐름) 음악의 발상지, 항상 국제적인 무대가 되고 있으며 세계 3대 미항중의 하나, 카니발과 삼바의 도시, 콜로니얼 풍의 건물등 다채롭고 화려한 모습을 하고 있다는 세계적인 관광도시가 후끈한 무더운 바람과 함께 우리를 반긴다.

가이드의 안내를 받으며 관광버스에 올라 바람에 살랑이는 야자수를 스치며 달려 코바카나바 해변이 확 펼쳐진 멋진 호텔에서 짐을 풀었다.

첫날은 자유시간으로 우리 일행은 중국식당에서 시원한 맥주를 음료수에 곁들여 포식하고 모두가 수영복으로 갈아입고 해변가로 달려나갔다.

철썩거리며 흰거품을 몰고오는 파도속에 묻혀 수영을 즐겼고 인파속에 파고드는 갈매기떼들과 코발트색의 찝찔한 바다내음과 총천연색 파라솔로 펼쳐진 수많은 인파속 백사장을 걸으며 남미의 정취를 만끽하면서 추억 만들기에 바빴다.

해가 서산으로 기우는 시간에 우린 호텔로 가 옷을 갈아입고 곧 바로 브라질의 유명한 삼바쇼를 관람키위해 서둘러 갔다. 휘황찬란한 의상과 눈부신 조명아래 펼쳐지는 음악과 삼바춤은 본고장의 멋을 흠뻑 쏟아내듯 아주 정열적이었다.

다음날 리오 데 자네이로의 정신적 지주라 할 수 있는 상질물 예수동상이 있는 코르코바도 언덕을 찾았다. 전동차로 해발 710m 정상에 올라 19세기 리오를 수호하며 브라질 독립 100주년을 기념하여 세워진 높이 30m, 양팔길이 28m의 거대한 예수동상 앞에 섰다. 도시 위로 불쑥 솟아있는 예수 그리스도의 동상은 얼마나 장엄하든지.

활짝 편 양팔은 사랑으로 모두를 감싸듯 마음 마저 폭은함을 갖게 한다.

어떻게 이 높은 산위에 동상을 세울 수 있었을까.

아래로 펼쳐진 풍경은 한 폭의 그림, 보고 또 보고를 얼마나 했는지.

다음 코스는 슈가로프 빵 산, 케이블카로 절반쯤 오르고는 첫 정거장에 내려 또 다른 케이불카를 갈아타고야 정상에 오를 수 있는 험한 코스인데, 정상에서 사방을 내려다보는 경관은 어떻게 말이나 글로 표현할 수 있을까 싶은 황홀함이었다. 또 그 높은 산위에 어울리지 않게 대나무 숲으로 꽉 메운 산책코스는 완전 정글로 이어진 오솔길로서 얼마나 정겹던지. 대나무 숲이 내뿜는 자연의 냄새에 마냥 취하기도 했다.

13.9km의 길이를 자랑하는 세계 최장의 니떼로이 해상교, 그림같이 해

상에 떠있는 멋진 요트들, 세계에서 가장 크다는 유명한 마라까낭 축구장은 마침 수리중이어서 아쉬움만 남겼다. 매년 2월에 열린다는 삼바 카니발 축제때는 15팀이 출전하는데 한 팀에 5,000명이 참가한다고 한다. 그 어마어마한 카니발 삼바거리를 걸어보는 동심의 세계를 맛보기도 했다.

브라질의 제2도시 리오에서의 짧은 스케줄로 많은 아쉬움이 남았지만, 일정에 따라 내일은 마음 설레게하는 세계 제일의 폭포 '이과수'를 향해 이동하는 날이다. 밤새도록 호텔 베란다 슬라잉 도어를 활짝 열어놓고 철썩거리며 들려오는 코바카나바 해변의 파도소리를 자장가 삼아 잠을 청했다.

다음 날 아쉬움을 남기고 브라질 제2의 도시 리오를 떠나 비행기로 이과수를 향해 날아갔다. 3시간만에 이과수 공항에 도착했다. 공항을 벗어나는 길목은 한적한 시골풍경으로 이곳에 세계 제1의 폭포가 있다니 믿어지지 않았다.

브라질 이과수 폭포앞에서

한참을 달려 브라질, 아르헨티나, 파라과이 3국 국경이 마주보이는 브라질 쪽에 섰다. 그리 넓지않은 빠나나강을 건너는 배 한 척이 아르헨티나를 향해 유유히 흘러간다.

촉촉히 뿌려대던 비도 잠시, 금세 화창한 여름 태양이 더운 공기를 뿜어댄다.

브라질 전통 음식점에서 먹은 점심은 맛은 물론 멋스러움이 풍기는 이색적이며 낭만적 분위기가 물씬 묻어나 좋았다. 소, 돼지, 닭고기를 뾰족한 긴 꼬챙이에 끼워 로스구이해 웨이츠레스들이 손님의 접시마다 원하는 부위를 일일이 썰어주는 친절과 브라질산 붉은 와인을 맛보기도 했다.

다음 날 1541년에 발견, 1939년 국립공원으로 지정되고, 아르헨티나(1984년), 브라질(1986년)에서 각각 유네스코가 정한 세계문화재로 등록된 이과수 폭포로 향했다. 브라질, 아르헨티나, 파라과이 국경에 자리한 이과수 폭포는 북미 나이아가라, 아프리카 빅토리아와 함께 세계 3대 폭포로 불리며, 이구(Igu)는 '물', '아수(Assu)는 크고 위대하다' 는 뜻이 담겨있는 원주민 말로는 '거대한 물' 이라고 불린다. 285개의 크고 작은 폭포가 말굽 모양으로 굽이치는 거대한 폭포로 전체 넓이는 총 4km, 우기에는 초당 1만3천톤의 물이 쏟아져 내린다고 한다. 80여m 의 낙차에 분당 1만톤 이상의 물을 뿜어내면서 물보라와 웅장한 음향을 발산한다.

폭포로 가는 산책로에는 '과치'라 불리는 꼬리가 긴 너구리과의 동물이 관광객을 반긴다. 노랑, 주홍색 등 갖가지 빛깔로 몸을 단장한 수천마리의 나비떼들이 여기저기서 낙엽이 바람에 날리듯한 신비한 모습에 넋을 빼앗기기도 했다.

마꾸꼬 사파리 투어를 위해 찝차를 타고 밀림의 정글로 들어섰다.우거진 울창한 나무숲사이로 간혹 햇빛이 방긋 보이기도 하고 들짐승들은 재빠르게 눈치채며 숨기도 한다. 선착장에 도착, 우비와 구명조끼를 입고 20여명이 보트를 타고 마치 파노라마 사진을 보는듯한 수십 개의 폭포가 펼치는 장관 속으로 접근해갔다.

곡예운전에 여행자들의 환호성은 높아가고 막상 큰 폭포로 접근하는 순간 심장의 고동소리가 귀에 들릴 만큼 스릴도 배가 되고, 눈도 뜨지 못할 정도의 물벼락에 정신이 없었다. 우비 무장은 필요도 없이 흠뻑 젖은 생쥐꼴이 되었다.

1991년에 폭포 아래쪽에 세워진 세계 최대 수력발전소인 '이따이푸 댐'으로 갔다. 아르헨티나, 브라질 전력사용량 40%을 생산하는 어마어마한 댐을 보고, 국경을 넘어 아르헨티나에 위치한 이과수 폭포 최고 하이라이트인 악마의 목구멍으로 갔다. '쉭쉭' 거친 소리를 내며 물이 떨어졌다가 다시 하늘로 솟구친다는 이 모습이 마치 악마가 숨 쉬는 것과 비슷하다고 해서 지어진 이름이란다. 떨어지면 헤어 나올 수 없는 폭포. 난간을 꽉 잡고 서서 엄청난 굉음을 질러대며 물기둥을 내리꽂는 웅장한 세계 제일의 폭포를 바라보면서, 어마어마한 대자연의 숭고한 입김 앞에 한없이 초라한 인간의 삶을 다시 한번 음미해보는 시간이기도 했다.

다음 날 브라질 이과수 공항을 이륙, 2시간 만에 탱고와 정열의 나라, 남미의 파리로 불리는 아르헨티나의 수도 부에노스 아이레스에 도착했다. 공항을 벗어나 시내로 들어가는 도로변은 시야가 확 트이게 풍요로운 푸르름이라는 첫인상으로 다가온다. 건물 사이사이 공터마다 왁자지껄 청소년들의 공차기가 한창 축구의 나라 브라질 이웃나라 답다.

부에노스 이이레스는 라폴라타 강의 서쪽, 대서양에서 240km 떨어진 곳에 자리 잡고 있는데 1880년 연방수도로 확정됐다. 인구 1,200만명, 세계에서 8번째로 큰 나라, 국민소득 5,100불, 관광이 넘쳐나는 도시, 교민도 2만 명이 훨씬 넘는단다.

인파로 북적거리는 백화점이 바로 코앞에 있는 한 호텔에 짐을 풀었다. 도로에 펼쳐진 꽃밭처럼 네온사인과 하늘로 올라간 빌딩 창문마다 화려한 불꽃송이가 하나 둘 켜질 무렵, 우리는 탱고 디너쇼를 관람키 위해 은근한 조명 속 극장으로 들어섰다. 붉은 포도주를 곁들인 전통 음식을 먹으며 환한 무대 위에 오른 젊은 남녀무희들이 펼치는 탱고는 어찌나 정열적이고 흥겹든지 몸을 온통 좌우로 흔들어 놓는다.

다음날 최고 43층 등 고층건물이 즐비한 널찍한 상가와 극장이 넘쳐나는 돌로 포장된 좁은 고풍의 거리로 나섰다. 어둠이 뿌려지면 결코 잠들지 않는다는 거리, 마치 벌집을 터트려 놓은 것 같은 인파 속 거리에 우뚝 서 있는 1810년 독립혁명이 일어난 5월의 광장과 접해있는 핑크벽돌의 대통령궁은 대대적인 보수로 인부들의 손놀림이 바쁘고, 국회의사당과 생각하는 사람 조각상이 나란히 조화를 이루고 있다.

보까('입'이란 뜻)지역은 아르헨티나의 탱고의 발상지, 이곳 사람들에게 탱고는 그저 생활의 일부분이다 라고 증명하듯 햇빛 찬란한 거리거리마다 탱고춤을 추는 남녀무희들, 넘쳐흐르는 탱고가락은 한바탕 춤을 추고 싶도록 애절하게 또는 끈끈하게 감아돌며 발걸음을 멈추어 놓는다,

10~20마리의 개들을 산책시키느라 무리지어 몰고 다니는 수많은 개들의 훈련사들을 쉽게 볼 수 있는 이색적인 도시.

돌로 견고하게 지어진 무덤. 레꼴레타(Recoleta) 국립묘지는 200년의 역사를 지닌, 마치 아파트단지를 방불케 하는 초호화판 묘지다. 정문을 배경으로 멋스럽게 펼쳐져있는 200년이 넘는 희귀한 고무나무가 한몫해 사랑받는 거리로 불리는 이웃만큼 규모가 대단하다. 그 유명한 에비타의 묘소, 그녀의 가족묘지가 여기에 있다. 골목골목에서 풍기는 야릇한 냄새가 코를 자극한다. 그녀가 묻힌 묘역은 시내에 있는 관광 일번지로 많은 꽃들이 놓여있다.

에비타 페론(Evita Eva Peron)은 이 나라에서 예수였다.

매춘부, 3류 가수에서 혁명가로 대통령 영부인까지 신데렐라같은 운명의 여인으로 살다가 예수와 같은 나이 33살에 암으로 죽은 전설적 여인, 서민의 대모, 마리아로,. 아르헨티나 국민들에게 그녀를 향한 연민의 정은 대단하다.

다음날 도시를 벗어나 녹색으로 펼쳐진 목장에 도착, 마차를 타고 승마를 즐기기도 했다. 이국의 낭만과 정취에 흠뻑 젖어본 브라질 리오에서 아르헨타나 남미의 파리까지 8박 9일동안 삶의 보람과 추억의 사진첩을 엮는 기쁨을 주신 하나님께 감사하며, 여행은 때때로 고생도 따르기도 하지만 돌아가 쉴 수 있는 나의 집이 있다는 것이 얼마나 행복인가.

밤이 깊은시간, 미국. 나의 집이 있는 워싱턴을 향해 비행기는 요란한 소리를 내며 높이높이 상공으로 오르고 있었다

아테네 그리고 신비의 카파도키아(Cappadocia)에서

아테네는 그리스의 수도로 전 인구의 약 절반인 400만 명이 사는 정치, 경제, 문화의 중심지다. 나라는 무너져도 자기는 살아야 된다는 나라. 그래서 Tax가 없는 나라. GNP 17,000불로 속으로는 잘 사는 나라다.

뉴욕에서 출발, 9시간 반 만에 아테네에 도착했다. 시내로 들어가는 길목에는 세계최고 산지답게 올리브나무가 즐비하고 불어오는 바람에 싱그러운 물결을 이룬다. 골목길 노상카페에서 간단한 요기를 하고, 에기나 해 해변가도를 위험천만하게 달리는데 해상에는 짓푸른 에멜랄드색 바다에 가지각색 요트가 한 폭의 그림이다.

오나시스와 재클린의 로맨스의 현장이다. 그리스 남성은 나이 80이 되어도 정열적인 남성미가 넘친다고 가이드가 목청을 높인다. 500만 불이 넘는 호화별장들이 줄지어 자리해 있다.

그날은 콘돌리사 라이스 미국 국무장관의 아테네 공식 방문 일정에 끼어 시내 곳곳이 막히는 바람에 우리 스케줄에 차질이 생겼다. 오후가 돼서야 아테네 시내로 들어가 신다그마 광장(최초로 헌법을 선포한 곳) 근대 올림픽경기장, 무명용사의 묘, 국회의사당등 시내관광을 했다. 둘째 날은 2시간가량 달려 고린도에 도착, 세계 3대 운하인 고린도 운하와 고린도 고대유적, 사도 바울이 갇혔던 감옥, 세례 받던 연못을 둘러봤다. 기원전 7세기경 고린도는 무역도시로서 최전성기를 맞았다는데 고린도의 항아리가 세계 각지에 존재하고 있는 것으로 증명되고 있다.

유명한 아폴로 신전이 이곳에 있다. 아테네로 돌아와 1973년 유네스코 투표 세계문화재 1호인 파르테논 신전(처녀의 집)을 찾았다. 민주주의 철학, 문화, 예술을 꽃피웠으며, 사도 바울이 기독교 선교를 위해 연설한 곳이며 휴머니즘의 발상지였단다. 아크로폴리스 언덕을 오르며 아테네 시내 야경을 내려다보며 곳곳에 숨어있는 역사의 숨결을 듣는 것 같았다.

셋째 날에는 피레우스 항으로 이동, 크르즈 배를 타고 지중해의 가장 아름다움을 자랑하는 에기나, 이드라, 로도스섬을 찾았다. 낭만과 환상의 섬이라 말하고 싶다. 선내에서 그리스 전통무용과 음악을 곁들인 쇼를 관람하며 무대에 나가 함께 춤을 추며 우리 가요 「만남」 을 밴드에 맞추어 부르는 영광(?)을 누리기도 했다.

다음날 아테네를 출발, 6시간을 달려 메데오라에 도착했다. 구멍이 뺑뺑 난 희귀한 바위산들, 뾰족산들과 기암절벽들을 봤다. 낮은 곳은 20~30미터, 높은 곳은 400미터나 되는 바위 탑, 기묘한 모양을 한 바위 위에 서있는 수도원, 그 유명한 007영화 촬영 현장이다. 어떻게 저런 뾰족 바위산에 멋진 수도원을 지을 수 있었을까, 모두들 감탄을 연발하며 사방에서 카메라를 들고 법석이다. 모두 24개의 수도원이 세워졌지만 현재 사용하는 수도원은 6개 뿐인데 최대의 수도원은 메가로 메테오론 수도원이다 . 여자들은 치마를 입어야 들어 가는곳, 바지를 입은 여자들을 위해 수도원 입구에서 치마를 빌려 주고 있다.

데살로니가로 이동 했다. 그리스 제2도시로 인구 약70만 명. 쎄르마이코스만이라는 좋은 항구가 있어 상공업의 중심지로 발전하고 있다. 현대적인 건물에 섞여 고대 비잔틴시대의 건물이 분위기를 만들어내고 있다. 18~19세기의 터키 시대에는 감옥으로 사용되었던 '피로 물든 탑' 이라고 불리는 화이트타워가 자리잡고 있고, 데살로니카 고고학 박물관과 그리스 최대의 교회 아기오스 디미트리오스 교회가 있다. 그리스의 마지막 밤 호텔식당에서 유명한 그리스의 붉은 포도주로 건배를 들었다. 내일은 터키를 향해 그리스 키피 국경을 넘는다.

이른 새벽 잠에서 덜 깬 몸들을 추슬러 호텔 문을 나섰다. 대기 중인 버스를 타고 넓은 고속도로를 달린다. 들판엔 목동이 이끄는 수많은 양떼들의 행렬이 평화와 낭만을 부르고, 집시들이 모여사는 울긋불긋한 천막촌 앞에서 손흔드는 집시어린아이들, 그리고 언덕에 늘어서 있는 크고 작은 주택들. 붉은 지붕마다 태양열을 이용하는 솔라(Solar)장치가 특이하다. 어느새 그리스 키피 국경을 넘어 터키의 넓은 고속도로를 달린다.

간간이 뿌려대던 빗방울도 그치고 맑게 개인 화창한 날씨가 카파도키아 기암 능선을 평면의 수목화처럼 그려내고 있는 곳에 도착했다. 카파도키

아는 문명의 교차로인 소아시아, 터키의 땅 한복판에 자리하고 있다.

기암의 절벽 아래를 내려다 보니 '와 와' 탄성 소리가 절로 새어 나온다. 카파도키아는 딴 세상이다. 떠돌이 행성 위를 거니는듯 꿈속이나 만화에서 볼 수 있는 이상한 들판 위에 섰다. 그야말로 공상 속의 풍경 같다. 버섯모양의 바위가 불쑥 솟았고 아이스크림 콘 같은 바위가 떼를 이뤘다. 그 기암마다 스위스 치즈 같는 구멍이 나있는데 이는 창문이고 테라스다. 누가 만든 작품이고 그곳에 살던 이는 또 누구였을까. 질문이 마구 내 마음을 흔들어댄다.

이 기괴한 풍경은 1,000만년 시간이 빚은 예술, 화산이 폭발해 용암이 흐르고, 또 다른 화산의 새 용암이 덮고 또 덮어 땅으로 굳어진 것을 바람이 깎고 빗물이 훑어내며 만들어낸 조각들이다. 어떻게 글로, 말로 정확히 표현할 수 있을까. 유네스코 지정 세계문화 자연 복합 유산인 카파도키아의 기암 풍경을 둘러보는 중심지는 괴레메다. 이곳을 중심으로 위르귭, 아바노스 등을 둘러보는 것이 가장 일반적인 관광코스. 괴레메 야외 박물관은 기암의 모습도 볼만하지만 그 안에 꾸며진 암굴 교회로 유명한 곳으로 기암석 교회만도 10여 개에 달한다. 벽화의 특징 등에 따라 애플교회, 뱀교회, 다크교회 등으로 불린다. 겉모습과 달리 실내에 장식된 화려한 프레스코화들이 당시 교인들의 신심을 짐작케 한다.

괴레메의 우치사르 언덕과 비둘기계곡은 기암을 펼쳐놓은 풍경이 장쾌

하고 포도밭으로 둘러싸인 파샤바흐의 기암은 꼭 거대한 남근석을 닮아 바라보기도 민망할 지경이다. 카파도키아는 전략적 요충지로 고대부터 잦은 싸움이 일어났던 곳이다. 사람들이 전란을 피해 몸을 숨겼던 곳이 바로 이 기암들이었다. 바위는 사암보다 부드러워 속을 파내기가 수월할 것같다.

깊은 우물(deep well)이란 뜻의 데린쿠유에 가면 벌판 아래 거대한 지하도시를 만난다. 기암 속이 아닌 땅속에 꾸며놓은 피난처다. 지하8층 구조로 50m까지 내려간 지하도시로 통로가 좁고 천장이 낮고 층계가 많아 오르내리느라 진땀이 흐른다. 호흡도 쉽지 않다. 종교의 박해를 피해 숨어든 초기 기독교인들의 자취를 둘러보면서 밝은 햇볕을 한번도 보지 못하고 처참하게 살다간 그들의 삶을 생각하면 가슴에 찡한 눈물이 흐른다.

그리스, 터키의 역사가 살아 숨쉬는 명소를 둘러보면서, 특히나 카파도키아의 신비로운 풍경에 감탄하며, 본질적인 나의 삶을 되돌아보게 하는 기회 주심과 건강 허락하여 주신 하나님께 감사 드린다.

아프리카 세네갈에 가다

한때 세상을 풍미했던 「뿌리」의 주인공 킨타 쿤테의 나라, 사하라 사막 끝자락 아프리카 대륙 최서단에 위치한 세네갈로 단기 선교를 갔다. 뉴욕을 경유, 9시간을 날아 수도 다카르(Dakar) 국제공항에 도착했다. 프랑스의 식민지였으며 1960년에 독립한 나라다. 공항밖으로 나오니 새벽인데도 뜨거운 열기가 대단하다.

우린 짐과 함께 두 차에 올라 울퉁불퉁한 길로 엉덩방아를 찧어가며 어둠이 깔린 새벽길을 달려갔다. 우리는 11박 12일간 단기 어린이 VBS 선교사역 목적을 띠고 세네갈의 오지로 온 것이다.

우리 일행은 다음날 아침 찝차로 솥뚜껑 같은 지붕을 이은 토담집이 옹기종기 모여 있는 오지 '음부르' 마을로 들어갔다. 전기도 없고 문명의 혜택이 전혀없는 곳이다.

우리 일행을 보고 많은 아이들이 손을 흔들며 뛰어 왔다. 400여 명이 순식간에 모였다. 물이 없어 씻지 못해 땟국물에 범벅이 된 채 머리에는 종기(부스럼)가 나 진물이 흐르는 많은 어린아이들, 팬티를 입지 않아 달랑 내놓고 누나 곁에서 앉아 졸고 있는 아이, 캔디를 하나 더 달라고 조르는 어른들과 아이들, 아이가 아이를 업고 땀을 뻘뻘 흘리며 서 있다.

'천지창조' '아기 예수님의 탄생' '예수님을 만나 변화된 삭게오' 등의 융판에다 예쁜 그림을 붙여가며 한국어, 세레어, 월로프어 3개 언어 통역으로 이어지는 이야기에 귀 기울이며 검은 피부에 하얀 이를 드러내고 손뼉치며 찬양하는 모습이 얼마나 축은하든지 눈물이 흐른다.

우리나라의 1950~1955년 전후를 상상하면 꼭 맞을 것 같은 환경이다. 돼지, 닭, 염소, 양들이 온 동네를 누비고 다니는 동물과 사람이 함께 공존하는 삶을 본다. 나귀가 이끄는 마차를 타고 어디론지 달려가는 전통의상 '부 부'를 입은 어른들, 삐쩍 마른 소떼를 몰고 다니는 목동들, 큰 웃물에 두레박을 드리고 퍼낸 물을 항아리에 담아 머리에 이고 조심스럽게 걸어가는 여인들, 모래밭에 파릇한 어린 싹이 애타게 비를 기다리는 무더움에 시들함이 애잔하다.

전통음식 '야샤 뿔레(Yassa Poulet)'를 함께 먹으며 현지인들과 쌀라 말레쿰? (안녕하세요?) 말레쿰 살람? (네! 안녕하세요?) 서로 주고받는 인사속에 정이 듬뿍 들었다. 모여온 아픈 사람 중에는 한쪽 다리가 썩어가는 중년부인이 있었다.

약을 바르고 치료하는 선교사님과 사모님의 모습을 바라보며 선교는 돌아봄이요 나눔의 시작이 아닌가 생각하며 너무 많이 누리고 있는 우리들의 모습을 회개하는 시간이기도 했다. 봉사활동을 마치고 '생고르' 마을을 떠나오는 날 끝까지 흔들어주던 그들의 여린 손들이 눈에 선하다.

다카르 현지 집사님댁에서 오랫만에 그리고 그리던 찬물 샤워를 하고 냉장고에 넣어둔 시원한 망고를 먹었다. 비행기 시간까지 몇 시간 남은 동안 다카르 앞바다의 고레 섬(Gor Island)을 들러봤다. 노예사냥에 포획된 흑인들이 미주로 팔려가기 전에 수용되었던 섬이다. 유네스코에서 인류문화유산으로 지정한 곳이기도 하다.

마치 우마처럼 한곳에 모아두고 몸무게를 달아서 경매를 붙이고 값을 매겨 팔아치우던 노예시장. 그 곳에는 아직도 그들을 강금했던 방과 체력검사를 하던 장소가 생생이 남아있다. 바다 쪽으로 자그마한 문이 하나 나 있다.

그 문을 통해 팔과 다리에 철갑을 두른 노예들은 배에 실리고 마침내는 멀고도 험한 대서양을 건너 신세계로 팔려갔다.

두 시간 정도의 섬 방문을 마치고 오백년도 더 살았다는 느티나무를 꼭 닮은 바호바 나무 아래서 잠시 쉬면서 생각해보았다. 슬픈 노예들의 비참했던 그때의 그 상황들을. 바호바 나무는 낱낱히 기억하리라 인간의 잔인함을….

알래스카 여행

늘 가보고 싶었던 곳, 한여름에 무더위를 식힐 수 있는 곳, 미국 어느 관광지보다 경비가 많이 든다는 곳. 미국의 모든 명소를 다 보고 맨 나중 여행하자는 남편의 계획에 순종하듯 이제야 알래스카를 찾았다. 5박 6일 여행에 필요한 것들, 특히 여행지가 춥다니 두툼한 재킷도 찾아 정성껏 백을 쌌다. 남편은 두 개로 나누지 왜 큰 백에다 모두 다 넣었냐고 투정이다. 9·11 이후 공항검색이 심한 걸 감안해서 했는데 말이다. 그래서 이 백은 여행기간 전적으로 내가 책임진다고 마음먹고 공항으로 달렸다. 그래도 차를 공항 주차장에 세우고 셔틀버스에 오르면서 백을 들고 쩔쩔 매는 나를 보고는 금방 남편이 백을 들어줬다. 모른 척하고 슬그머니 맡겨버렸다.

밤 11시가 넘어 앵커리지 공항에 도착했다. 호텔로 가니 밤11시가 훨씬 넘었는데 밖은 여전히 환한 백야다. 정말 미국이란 나라가 얼마나 넓은지 별천지에 온 느낌을 갖게 했다. 다음날부터 본격 관광에 나섰다. 유람선을 타고 3시간 여를 미끄러지듯 흘러가니 깎아지른 듯한 빙벽이 앞을 가로막아 선다. 두둥실 떠있는 흰 구름에 잉크를 잔뜩 뿌려 번진 듯한 빙벽의 일부분이 갑자기 물밑으로 떨어지며 쏟아내는 얼음 파편과 굉음에 탄성이 절로 난다. 빙하가 서서히 녹으면서 높은 얼음산에서 폭포가 되어 떨어지는 소리 또한 그 자체가 우렁찬 자연의 신비로움이었다. 갑판에서 차갑게 불어대는 바람을 맞으며 '타이타닉' 영화 주인공 제스추어도 흉내내 본다. 연어 떼들이 물위로 겁 없이 튀어오르는 광경도 너무나 멋지다.

다음날 우린 9인승 프로펠라 경비행기를 타고 디날리 국립공원으로 달렸다. 맥켄리의 험악한 바위산과 눈 덮인 산들을 내려다보며 어미곰과 아기곰의 나들이, 뿔달린 사슴떼들이 펼치는 동물의 세계를 공중에서 만끽할 수 있었고, 등반사고로 지금도 빙하에 묻혀 있다는 고상돈, 이일교 씨의 기념무덤도 찾아가 볼 수 있었다.

다음날에는 디스커버리 증기유람선을 탔다. 개썰매들의 행진이 멋지게 이어지고 연어 잡는 방법과 처리과정을 봤다. 사금 채취장에서는 우리 손으로 직접 채취한 금으로 예쁜 목걸이를 만들어 목에 걸었다. 또 거대한 산맥을 뚫고 바다속 터널을 거쳐 육지위로 꾸불꾸불 큰 구렁이 모양 이어지는 800마일의 원유 수송파이프라인을 보면서 인간의 노동력이 얼마나 위대한가를 느낄 수 있었다.

백야의 골프도 쳤다. 워낙 추운 곳이라 그린은 좋지 않았지만 밤 8시에 티업해 날이 바뀌어 1시반까지 골프치는 묘미는 남달랐다. 해가 넘어가니 엄청나게 춥다.

점퍼를 안 가져갔으면 모두가 동태가 될 뻔했다. 독립기념일이 끼어있어 사방에서 불꽃놀이가 시작되었지만, 하늘로 치솟는 소리와 연기만이 있을 뿐 환한 밤에 아름다운 불꽃을 볼 수는 없었다. 훼어뱅크스에서 앵커리지까지 가는 장장 10시간이 넘는 길은 강원도의 대관령 미시령을 연상케 한다. 꼬불꼬불 아슬아슬함에 가슴 조이고 하늘을 찌를듯 우뚝우뚝 솟은 산을 온통 덮은 하얀눈과 계곡마다 채워진 얼음바다가 눈을 부시게 했다. 마지막날 알래스카 역사박물관을 보고 알래스카 특산 연어포를 샀다. 손자, 손녀 선물로 하얀 곰인형도 샀다.

여행중 만난 일본 여자의 충고대로 특별히 요청해 마운틴 사이드 창문쪽에 운좋게 앉을 수 있었다. 솜이불을 펴놓은듯 가지런히 깔린 구름을 뚫고 솟아나 있는 뾰족산은 정말 장관이었다. 이번 여행은 다름아닌 나의 환갑여행, 두달을 앞당겨 딸들이 서둘러 만들어준 축하여행이었다. 정 많은 딸들이 늘 보채듯 애기하는대로 건강하고 늙지않는 엄마가 되도록 노력해야겠다.

일본에서의 6박 7일

일년 전 우리는 747 대한항공을 타고 시속 570마일로, 망망대해 태평양 위를 조금도 흔들림 없이 흰구름을 헤치며 일본을 향해 날아갔다. 1972년에 지었다는 나리타공항에 착륙, 입국수속을 마치고 현지 가이드의 마중을 받으며 우리 일행은 대기중이던 작으마한 버스에 탑승 65Km 떨어진 동경을 향해 뉘엿뉘엿 기우는 석양빛을 바라보며, 레인보우Bridge를 건너 다닥다닥 붙은 빌딩숲을 지나 좁은 도로를 헤쳐가며 신주쿠시 중심가에 위치한 한 호텔에 짐을 풀었다.

가이드의 안내로 동경도청 전망대에 올라가 휘황찬란한 동경의 밤 시가지를 동서남북으로 방향을 바꾸어가며 바라보았다. 멀지 않은 곳에 50년의 역사를 자랑 하는 높이 3776m의 동경타워가 멋진 불빛을 내뿜으며 우뚝 서 있다. 호텔로 돌아온 우린 호텔 방에 그냥 쉰다는 것이 너무 아까워 남편과 난 무작정 밖으로 나가 활기차게 활보하는 행인들과 합류하여 걷기 시작했다.

기모노 입은 여인들이 아장아장(?) 우리 곁을 속삭이며 기나간다 .혹시나 호텔을 잃을까, 길 이름을 외우고 화려한 신주쿠의 밤거리를 걸으며 지하철 상가로 내려갔다. 스시집, 빵집, 우동집 등 그야말로 먹거리로 꽉 차 있고 거리마다 '욘사마' 탈렌트 배용준의 사진이 대문짝만하게 붙어있어 일본에서 그의 인기가 대단함을 읽을 수 있었다. 밤 11시가 훨씬 넘었는데도 거리마다 식당마다 까만 양복 차림의 젊은이들로 넘친다.

다음날 동경 시내로 관광을 나섰다. 그들의 '신'이 머물러 있다는 명치신궁, 흰옷, 검정 제복차림의 제사지내는 모습과 결혼식을 막 끝낸 신랑신부가 전통 의상을 갈아입어 가며 사진 촬영하는 것이 너무 인상적이라 많은 관광객이 축하의 환호성을 지르며 그들과 사진 찍기에 바빴다. 아사쿠사관음사로도 불리는 센소사, 그리고 말썽 많은 고이즈미 총리가 전범자 원혼을 위한 신사 참배하던 야스쿠니신사를 관람했다. 주위엔 선물가게가 즐비하게 늘어서 있다.

1603년에 지어진 125대 아키히토 천왕과 황태자가 살고 있는 황궁으로 갔다. 면적이 30만평(300에이커) 돌담이 쳐 있고 빙 둘린 호수가에는 두 마리의 백조가 유유히 물가를 맴도는 그림이

너무 보기 좋았다. 길이 29m의 이중교는 철교와 석교로 견고함이 돋보이며, 현재의 천왕은 꼭둑각시에 불과하며, 황궁은 천왕의 생일 12월 23일과 1월 1일 일년에 두번 개방 한다. 황궁 옆에는 국회의사당이 자리해 있다. 아키하바라 전자상가와 긴자의 번화가를 걸으며 미츠코시(Mitsukoshi)라는 긴자의 일류 백화점엔 손님이 밀려 불황을 모르는 것 같았다.

다음날 하코네로 이동, 산림이 우거진 경치 최고의 하코네 국립공원에 도착, 호화 유람선을 타고 둘레가 18Km 수심 41Km의 아시호수는 떠 있는 수많은 요트와 숲이 어우러져 한폭의 그림이다. 이 산 저 산에서 하얗게 무럭무럭 김이 솟아오르고 코를 찌르는 유황냄새가 흠뻑 젖은 오와쿠다니 유황 계곡에 케이불카를 타고 올라가 흰 계란을 끓는 유황물에 잠깐 넣었다 꺼내면 익고 검정 계란이 되는 이 검정계란을 먹으면 5살이나 젊어진다는 전설 같은 얘기에 관광객들은 계란 사먹느라 북적거린다

하코네를 벗어나 좁은 길로 꼬불꼬불 4시간이나 걸려 나고야에 도착 했다. 나고야는 중경도시 공업도시로 유명하고 사람들은 전형적 일본인들만 모여 산다. 다음 날 아침 복잡하고 정신없이 넓은 나고야역에 나가 신칸센 고속철을 타고 40분만에 교토에 도착했다. 교토는 인구 140만 명 일본에서 5번째로 꼽히는 도시로 7~8세기 까지 수도로써 기능을 하다 1868년 명치 유신 이후 문화 예술의 도시로 탈바꿈하여 대표적인 금각사와 청수사와 같은 멋지고 아름다운 문화유적지를 남겼다. 강이 많아 운치가 좋은 곳이라서 아름다운 여인과 여장부가 많이 배출된다는 곳, 씨름을 좋아해 일년에 써머(씨름) 대회가 6번이나 열린다. 특이한 것은 이 고장 사람은 5번 거절한 후에 응해야 예의가 있고 대접받는다고 하니 참으로 별스러운 고장 이다.

1,650개의 절과 400개의 신사가 있으며 지하철이 운행되고 있다. 교토를 벗어나면서 길가에 굵은 대나무밭이 빽빽이 들어서 있고 대나무는 지진에

많은 도움이 되어 곳곳마다 대나무를 많이 심어 놓은 것을 볼 수 있다. 나라(Nara)로 이동 1300년의 역사를 자랑하는 동대사, 이 절은 부처님 손바닥 위에 장정 18명이 올라가 서 있을 수 있는 어마어마한 크기의 부처님을 모신 큰절로 규모가 엄청나다. 옛날 가이사 대사란 분이 동대사로 올 때 사슴을 타고 왔기에 그 분을 기리기 위해 그 주위에 2,000마리의 사슴을 풀어놓고 기르고 있다. 이어 오사카로 이동했다.

오사카에는 재일교포가 35만명이 살고 있으며 오사카 사투리는 특이하고 거칠고 직설적이면서도 뒤끝이 없는 성격으로 코미디언이 많이 배출된다고 한다. 도요토미히데요시의 오사카 성을 외부에서 관람하고 쇼핑상가 밀집지역인 신사이바시에 있는 소니타워(SonyTowe)에 올라가 신제품을 눈요기하고 어둠이 깔릴 무렵, 우리는 오사카 남항부두로 이동, 관선기선 큰 훼리를 타고 2인 1실의 객실에서 잠자며, 13시간만에 일본 최대의 온천지인 뱃푸(Beppu)에 도착 했다.

싱그러운 야자수가 바닷바람에 살랑거리고 하얗게 뿜어대는 온천 김이 하늘로 피어오르는 광경, 빨건 진흙이 부글부글 끓어오르는 것이 마치 지옥 같아 '바다지옥'이란 이름이 붙은 이색적인 관광지며 문화재 속에 속해있다. 졸졸 대롱으로 흘러내리는 유황 섞인 물을 약수로 잘못 알고 마시고, 우리 일행은 한

때 걱정으로 초죽음(?)에 이르도록 웃지 못할 추억을 만들기도 했다.

유황성분으로 염색, 화학 원료로 쓰이는 명반(백반)재배 하는 움막에 들어가 재배하는 과정을 볼 수 있었다. 지하 200m~300m에서 솟구치는 90도~100도(화씨)이상의 온천에서 피로를 풀기도 하고, 수천 마리의 야생원숭이들이 모여 사는 '다카사키' 원숭이 공원에 올라가 새끼 원숭이들의 재롱에 쏙 빠지기도 하고, 뱃푸를 벗어나 '큐슈'에 도착, 까만 기왓장을 2층식으로 얹은 전통적인 집들로 옹기종기 모여 마을 전체를 이룬 시골마을을 돌아보았다. 전통 일본 소나무들과 큰 조각돌들로 정원마다 깔끔하게 잘 가꾸어 놓았다.

산자락에 펼쳐진 넓은 평원에 억새풀들이 바람에 한들한들 왈츠를 추고 한 켠엔 소떼들이 유유히 풀을 뜯는 낭만이 한껏 묻혀있어 마음까지 포근해졌다. '아소활화산분화구'는 안개가 많이 끼어 올라가지못해 아쉬움만 남기고 구마모토로 발길을 옮겼다. 박물관 구마모토성과 천수각은 가파른 층계로 되어있어 위험천만해 조심조심 오르내리며 관광 하느라 진땀 흘리며 고생하고. 마지막 날 야외 음악당을 겸비한 울창한 숲 속에 자리한 기가 막히게 멋진 호텔로 안내 해준다.

아마도 마지막날밤 일본여행 만큼은 아주 최고의 추억을 가지라고 마냥 인심을 쓴 것 같다. 모두들 온천을 즐기고 연두색과 흰색 바탕에 잔잔한 잎시귀가 수놓은 듯 조화를 이룬, 호텔에서 내준 똑 같은 유까다(잠옷)을 입고 그 위에 연두색 벨트를 느슨하게 여미고 쓰레빠(슬리퍼)를 신고 그대로 레스트랑에 내려가 와인을 마시며 저녁을 먹는 진풍경 속에 우리 부부도 예외 일 수가 없었다. 한테 어울려 식사하는 분위기는 전혀 달랐다. 오래전 부터 호텔 측에서 투숙 손님들을 편하게 모신다는 차원에서 적극 권장한다는 이색적인 이벤트로 꾸밈없는 신선한 모습에 매우 흥미로웠고 모두들 즐거워했다 .

어느새 6박 7일의 일본여행을 마치고 아침 일찍 우리 일행은 후쿠오카 공항으로 달린다. 흔들리는 차안에서 잠시 생각해본다. 주거비와 교통비 또한 물가가 비싼 나라 일본, 여행 중 환전하기 위해 은행에 갔었다 .엄청 더운 날이었다. 에어컨은 열심히 도는데 시원하지 않은데도 많은 손님들은 불평 안하고 부채질하며 절약 차원을 이해 하는 것 같고, 친절하고 국민들, 정치인 대다수가 13~15평 이내의 아파트에서 사는 절약형 국민성과 선조들이 남긴 수많은 유적지를 원형 그대로 잘 보존하여 많은 외화를 벌어들이는 검소한 나라라는 인상을 받고 느꼈다.

내 나라도 이에 못지 않을 거란 바람을 가지며 내 조국을 향하여 대한항공은 높은 창공으로 힘차게 올라 흰구름을 헤치며 날아갔다.

페루 선교를 다녀와서

리마에서 비행기로 1시간 반 비행하여 뚜루히요 공항에 도착했다. 뚜루히요는 페루의 수도 리마에서 북쪽으로 500마일 떨어져 있는 페루의 제3대 도시로 꼽힌다. 허나 공항은 어느 시골 버스 터미널 정도의 크기로, 뿌옇게 일어나는 흙먼지를 안고 우리 일행은 선교사집에 도착했다.

우리는 주로 빈민층을 위한 사역을 했다. 빈민층의 열약한 현지사정의 예를 들자면 세수할 물조차 사기 힘든 어려움과 하루에 한끼로 끼니를 이어야하는 가난함, 꾀죄죄한 땟국물이 범벅이 된 옷들을 입고 급식하는 날을 찾아 밥을 타먹기 위해 줄서서 기다리는 아이들의 눈빛이 얼마나 가엾어 보이든지. 현지 선교사님은 매주 수요일을 급식하는 날로 정하고 장작을 패서 밥과 닭찜을 만들어 배식 하는데 200여명이 몰려와 허겁지겁 먹는 모습을 보며 눈물이 핑 돌았다이 세상에는 이와 같이 굶주리는 아이들이 이곳만이 아닐텐데 지금까지 나는 너무 편한 삶 속에서 나만을 위한 삶을 살지 않았나 반성의 기회도 가지며 앞으로 더 많은 봉사를 해야겠다는 각오를 다져보았다.

이민가방에 가득가득 채워간 의약품을 가지고 리마에서 Trujillo로, Piura, Colan 등지를 다니며 현지 보건소장님도 나와 우리 선교팀과 함께 많은 환자를 돌보며 약을 나눠주며 그들의 고통을 덜어주는 일은 참 보람이 있었다. 또한 이발, 미용사를 겸해서 정말 내 남편 내 아이들의 머리를 깎는다는 그 이상의 사랑으로 정성 들여 깎아주며 매만져 주었다. 8살 미만의 어린아이들에게는 머리를 깎아주고는 예쁜 그림이 든 스티커를 손등에 붙여주고 볼펜과 노트를 나누어주며 좋아서 깔깔대는 천진스러움을 보면서 행복한 아이들의 천국을 맛보기도 했다.

소매치기 강도가 들끓는 가난한 사회 속에서 물들지 않고 우리 선교팀이 가르쳐준 주님의 성호를 율동을 곁들여 온몸으로 찬양하는 청소년들의 찬양집회가 얼마나 은혜스러웠든지. 우리 선교팀에게도 특송을 부를 기회가 있었다. "주 하나님 지으신 모든 세계"를 부르며 솟구치는 눈물을 참으며 주 하나님의 지으신 모든세계가 헐벗고 굶주리지 않고 전쟁과 테러가 없는 평화로움 속에서 살 수는 없는 것일까…

선교의 일원으로 봉사하면서 나 자신이 많은 은혜를 받았으며 가난한 현지 주민들에게도 무한한 하나님의 축복이 함께 하기를 기도 드리며 짧은 기간동안 안전하고 효율적인 선교를 이룰 수 있도록 인도하신 하나님께 감사드린다.

포르투갈 & 스페인 여행기

한여름이 되면 시원한 그늘을 드리우는 앞뜰의 나무 가지마다 조그맣게 꽃망울을 매달기 시작할 무렵 차곡차곡 정성껏 싸놓은 가방을 차에 싣고 워싱턴 덜레스공항으로 달려갔다. 독일 뮌헨을 경유, 총 10시간30분만에 리스본 공항에 도착했다.

포르투갈의 국토를 남북으로 가르며 흐르는 태주강(Rio Tejo)의 대서양 하구에 자리 잡고 있는 리스본은 남한보다 약간 작은 땅에 인구 85만의 포르투갈의 수도다. 리스본의 첫인상은 마치 출항하는 뱃머리에서 선 선장처럼 경쾌한 느낌이 든다. 리스본은 7개의 언덕으로 이루어진 노아의 손자가 정착한 나라라고도 한다.

2002년 월드컵 때 그라운드를 누비던 땀방울이 맺힌 피구의 얼굴과 박지성의 통쾌한 왼발 슛으로 얻은 승리의 감격이 아직도 생생이 남아있는 축구의 나라다. 리스본은 영어식 명칭이고 현지에서는 리스보아라고 통한다.

1755년 리스본 대지진으로 역사적 유적이 많이 손실되었고 폐허의 자리에 새로운 도시계획에 의한 신시가지가 조성된 차분하고 소박한 멋을 지닌 도시로서 곳곳에 전통 있고 웅장한 성당들이 많은 카톨릭 국가다.

첫번째로 달려간 곳은 유럽의 최서단이자 이베리아 반도의 땅 끝 마을인 카보다로카다. 포르투갈의 가장 서쪽 끝이자 유럽 대륙이 끝나는 곳. 볼거리나 유적보다는 이곳이 갖는 의미가 큰 곳으로 절벽에 와 부딪치는 대서양의 파도가 육지의 끝, 바다의 시작을 알린다. 거센 바람과 파도가 보는이들을 압도하는데 서쪽 끝에 있다는 황홀감을 느끼게 해주는 곳이다. "이곳에서 육지가 끝나고 바다가 시작되는구나" 라는 글귀가 적힌 시비가 바람을 맞으며 서 있다. 눈에 보이는 것은 우뚝 솟은 기념비와 휑한 자연이지만 파란 바다와 하늘이 구분하기 힘들어 예전에 CF 장소로 많이 애용됐다고 한다. 특히나 땅에 붙어있는 갖가지 색깔의 잔잔한 선인장 꽃들로 온통 뒤덮혀 너무나 특이한 멋을 풍겨준다.

100년~200년 된 건물들은 붉은 지붕을 얹고 고풍스러움과 예스러움이 묻어나는 골목길들이 도시의 역사를 묵묵이 일러주는 도시 전경 속에 매우 운치가 있는 전차도 달리고 있고 광장 곳곳마다 조각상이 홍수를 이루고 있다.

벨렘에 있는 장대한 고딕양식의 건물, 16세기 포르투갈의 전성기의 영광을 자랑하는 유네스코에 의해 세계 문화유산으로 지정된 제로니무스 수도원은 마침 미사 중이라 굳게 문이 닫혀있어 웅장한 수도원 건물을 배경으로 디카에 담으며 아쉬움을 달랬고, 가까운곳에 벨렘탑이 의젓하게 서 있어 들러보았다.

벨렘탑동쪽 저편 테주강 위에 세워진 '바스코다가마 다리' 는 테주강을 가로 지르는 길이 17km의 유럽에서 두번째 긴 다리로 일명 '4월25일교'라고도 하고, 리스본 하류에 놓인 전장 2,278m,교각 높이 190m로 마치 샌프란시스코에 있는 금문교와 흡사하다. 테주강은 스페인 중부에서 서쪽으로 흘러오는 길이 1,008 Km 이베리아 반도의 최장의 강으로 수많은 요트가 졸고있는 바닷가는 여유로운 풍경화를 그려내고 있다. 고메르시유광장과 로시우광장 사이에 놓인 아우구스타거리는 바이샤 최고의 쇼핑가로 맘편히 활보하는 명동같은 거리로 멋진 상점이 즐비하고 카페나 식당들이 많아 여행자들이 북쩍거린다.

로시오광장은 물결치는 듯한 광장바닥의 모자이크가 인상적이다. 기하학 무늬가 아름다운 화단이 조성되어 멀리 리스본시내와 테주강의 전경이 한눈에 들어오는 에드워드 7세 공원은 영국 에드워드 7세의 1902년 리스본 방문을 기념하여 프랑스식으로 조성된 녹색의 아름다운 공원으로 리스본관광의 하이라이트로 꼽히는 곳이다. 땅이 좁아 주차난 역시 심각한 상황이다. 주차된 차량의 범퍼를 자기차로 쿵쿵 밀어서 틈을 만든후 자기차를 세운다고 하니 온통 차들은 상처투성이다. 강바람과 바닷바람이 한데 섞여 불어오는 리스본 시내교통의 중심지 퐁발후작광장을 지나 상가에 불빛이 하나 둘 켜지는 어둠이 깔리는 시각에 리스본에서의 하루 관광을 마감하고 호텔로 갔다.

다음날 아침 리스본을 떠나 온통 올리브나무가 즐비한 국도를 달려 4시간 30분만에 플라맹고의 원조로 불리는 스페인의 4번째 큰도시 세비야에 도착했다. 인구 70만명으로 영어이름은 세빌리아로 부른다. 과달키비르 강변을 끼고 12각형의 모양을 갖춘 황금의 탑이 우뚝 서 있고 유람선이 강물따라 유유히 흘러가는 멋스러움이 마음을 사로잡는다. 다리를 건너 좁은 골목길로 접어들자 벌집과도 같은 많은 카페와 기념품가게가 넘쳐나고 관광객을 싣고 다니는 마차가 바쁘게 움직이는 낭만의 산타쿠르즈거리 앞에 웅장한 세비야 대성당이 견고한 모습으로 나타났다.

1401년~1519년에 완성된 세로 116m, 폭76m의 세비야 성당은 로마의 베드로 성당과 런던의 세인트폴 성당에 이어 세계의 3대성당으로 꼽힌다. 성당 뒷쪽으로 높이 97.5m, 전망대 높이 70m 를 갖춘 세비야의 상징이며 아름다움의 극치 이스람 사원이었던 히랄다탑(방향을 가르키는 닭)이 우뚝 솟아있다. 원래는 회교사원의 모스크 첨탑이었으나 16세기에 카톨릭 세력으로 청동 여신상을 덧붙여 올렸다며 기존의 건축물을 파괴하지않고 최대한 활용한 스페인사람들의 유연함을 설명하느라 가이드는 목청을 높인다. 첨탑에 오르고 싶었지만 시간이 맞지 않아 성당안으로 발거음을 옮겼다.

1.5톤의 금이 소요된 예수님의 생애를 조각한 세계 제일의 제단 병풍 앞에 서서 섬세한 작품에 감탄을 쏟아내며 세비야의 수호신인 성모상이 그려진 사원내 미술품을 감상하고 특히 4명의 스페인국왕이 사면에서 받들고 있는 아프리카 신대륙을 발견한 콜럼버스의 묘와 그가 바람피워 낳았다는 그의 아들의 묘를 보고 고개를 가웃거리면서도 관광객들은 사진 찍느라 법석이다.

스페인 광장

마리아 루이사 공원 안에 있는 스페인 광장으로 갔다. 중앙에는 하늘로 치솟는 분수가 장관이고 광장을 둘러싼 건물의 아치 아래에는 스페인 각지의 특성과 역사를 타일로 모자이

크한 그림같은 58개의 벤치가있다. 그 중에 마음에 드는 벤치에 앉아 디카에 담으며 세계적인 성악가 테너가수 '호세 카레라스'와 '플라시도 도밍고'의 조국에 온 보람을 갖기도 했다. 지중해 연안의 온화함 때문인가 고속도로 중앙 분리대 한가운데에는 리라꽃(라일락)이 흐드러지게 피어있어 얼마나 아름답든지.

우리가 잘 아는 베사메무쵸 노래 가사에 등장하는 바로 리라꽃 이기도 하다.

정열적인 집시여인 카르맨이 근무했다는 담배공장 건물옆을 지나며 비스크 지방의 순진한 돈 호세 하사와의 비극적인 사랑을 다룬 비제의 오페라 카르맨(Carmen)의 배경이 물씬 풍겨나는 도시에서 플라맹고를 직접 관람할 수 있다는 흥분속에 서둘러 극장으로 갔다. 상상외로 무대는 아주 작고 무희들의 빠른 손놀림과 화려하고 정열적인 춤과는 반대로 약간은 공허한 듯 하면서도 비장한 음색의 가수의 낭만보다는 삶의 고단이 느껴지고, 보편적 정서와 흥겨움보다는 아랍문화와 지역문화가 섞이고 절제와 낭만적 기질을 적절히 버무린 마음으로 추는 춤이라는 생각이 들기도했다. 세비야는 서고트왕국의 수도로 비제의 "카르멘" 로시니의 "세비야의 이발사" 등 숱한 오페라의 무대로 스페인 관광의 단골 메뉴. 특히 다른 나라에서는 찾아볼 수 없는 독특한 건축을 볼 수 있는 곳이기에 너무나 인상적이었다.

비가 간간히 뿌리는 날 세비야에서 버스로 이동. 2시간만에 시에라니아데 론다 산(698m) 언덕에 우뚝 선 작은 도시 론다에 도착했다. 인구 3만명의 이작은 도시는 스페인 안달루시아에서 가장 매력적이고 사랑스러운 도시 중 하나다. 론다로 가는 길은 대관령 넘어 동해로 가는 길과 흡사하며 사막처럼 아무 것도 없는 황량한 땅에 질서 정연한 올리브 나무가 비를 맞으며 싱그러움을 펼쳐내고, 1,500m 넘는 산을 굽이굽이 넘어가니 평지가 보이고 조금 후 저 멀리 요새같이 생긴 도시가 보인다. 과달레빈 강에 침식된 대지위에 알라메다 델 타호(Alameda del Tajo)에서 바라본 절벽과 18세기에 돌로 만든 다리로 한때 감옥으로 사용했다는 120m의 누에보 다리가 협곡사이에 아슬아슬한 자태를 뽐낸다. 과달레빈 강은 강줄기가 크지 않지만 절경과 어우러져 산수화를 그려놓고 있다.

론다에 있는 원조 투우장앞 (론다, 스페인)

스페인에서 가장 오래된 투우장이 있는 투우사들의 성지이기도 하다. 전설적인 인물로 기록되고 있는 투우사 페드로 로메로 는 생애를 통틀어 5,585마리의 소를 죽였고 자신은 몸에 상처 하나 남기지 않고 80세까지 여생을 즐겼단다. 헤밍웨이가 오랜시간 집필하면서 낭만을 즐겼던곳. 성 테레사 수녀가 기거했던 칼멘 수도원이 여기에 있다 오래된 기념품 가게를 기웃거리며 하얀벽 사이로 좁게 이어진 골목길을 걸었던 일은 론다에서 누렸던 소박한 기쁨중에 하나 였다.

생선요리로 점심을 먹고 우리는 론다를 떠나 2시간 만에 대서양과 지중해를 잇는 지브롤터 해협으로 들어가는데 여권 검사만으로 통과, 국경을 넘으니 눈앞에 영국국기가 펄럭이는것이 정말 영국령이란 게 실감난다. 비행기 활주로도 보이고 중간에 자그마한 예쁜 동네도 지나는데 거리거리에 사람들이 넘치고 상점들도 많다. 아주 비좁은 커브길을 운행해 올라가는데 스릴이 이만저만이 아니다. 운전사가 어찌나 익살을 부리는지 수많은 꼬리 없는 원숭이들이 조금 열어놓은 운전석 창문으로 손을 넣고 먹을 것을 달라고 재롱을 부린다. 규모가 단조로운 동굴을 구경하고 정상에 올라 지브롤터 시내와 항만을 내려다 보니 너무나 환상적이고 멋있고 아찔한 절벽이 스릴을 더해준다. 아프리카 대륙까지는 불과 15km로 맑은 날에는 모로코가 선명하게 보인다고 하는데 해변가에는 바람이 어찌나 센지 우뚝 서 있는 큰 등대와 멀리 지평선 모로코 쪽을 배경에 넣어 사진 찍는데 날아가지 않은 게 천만다행이었다.

오후 늦게 밝게 갠 햇살 아래로 코스타 델 솔(Costa del sol: 태양의 해변) 해변을 따라 마하스(Mijas: 하얗다)로 달려갔다. 오른쪽 코스타 델 솔 언덕엔 붉은 기와 기붕을 얹은 하얀집들이 눈부시고 왼쪽으론 코스타 델 솔 해변의 새파란 바다가 한 폭의 그림이 아닌가. 아! 감동 만발하는 사이 저기 산중턱에 눈에 띄는 하얀 마을 이정표 역시 마하스다 .

해질 무렵이 환상이라는데 마침 그 시간에 우린 호텔로 들어갔다. 발아래 펼쳐지는 마하스의 부촌들, 그 아래 너머로 보이는 코스타 델 솔해변. 여름이면 발 디딜 틈이 없이 세계 관광객이 몰리는 최고의 피서지로 유명한 곳 이란다. 정말이지 몇 날을 더 머무르고 싶었던 곳. 마하스의 하얀 거리에도 발그레한 벽돌로 물들이며 곳곳에 콘도건물들이 우뚝우뚝 증축되는 풍경을 펼쳐내고 있었다.

다음 날 아침 일찍 마하스를 떠나 항구도시 말라가(Malaga)도시에 도착했다. 복잡한 메르세드광장 한모퉁이에 자리잡고있는 현대 미술에 깊고도 큰흔적을 남긴 세계적인 화가 파불로 피카소(Picasso1881~1973)의 생가에 도착했다. 역시 화가였던 부친 호세 루이스부라스코의 유화와 피카소가 세례식때 입었던 의상과 사진들, 도자기, 조각등이 단조롭게 전시된 생가 내부를 관람하고. 우린 스페인의 꽃이라고 할 정도로 이슬람 문화가 살아있다는 그라나다(Granada :석류)로 이동했다.

그라나다의 대표적인 관광지인 세계 문화유산으로 지정되어 있는 유명한 알함브라 궁전(붉은 성벽)에 도착했다. 입구부터 조경이 너무나 멋져 호기심이 절로났다. 알함브라궁전의 성벽은 2km이고 길이가 740m에 달하는 하나의 단독건물이 아니라 메수알(Mexuar)궁전, 코미레스(Comares) 궁전, 사자(Leones)궁전, 나사렛 왕궁, 알카사바, 까들로스 5세 궁전 등이 합쳐진 궁전의 복합체로 석고와 대리석 가루를 틀에 찍어낸 정교하고 모든벽과 천정, 창문등이 화려한 글자와 세심한 문양으로 장식되어 있다. 감미로운 클래식기타의 선율로 인해 잘 알려진 14세기 이슬람 왕조 말기에 건축된 이스람 양식의 건축가들의 진수를 볼 수 있는 최고의 궁전이다.

124개의 대리석기둥이 둘러싸고 있는 가운데 12마리의 돌사자가 받치고 있는 분수의 사자정원 그리고 물소리까지 예술적으로 들리는 아세끼아의 정원은 아름다움의 극치라 할 수 있는 궁전을 관람하는데 2시간이 훨씬 넘게 걸렸다. 성벽에서 멀리보이는 아랍인들의 마을이었던 알바이신 지역을 관광하면서 언덕에 작으마한 동굴들을 파고 한집단을 이루고 사는 집시들의 마을이 애처롭게 눈에 들어왔다.

다음날 우린 스페인의 수도 마드리드로 이동중 어찌나 비가 쏟아지는지 마침 많은 시간을 차안에 있다는 행운속에 지나치는 국도변은 황토속의 밀밭과 포도밭 그리고 지중해에서 신이내린 선물로 불린다는 올리브 나무가 질서정연하게 온 벌판을 뒤덥은 차창밖 풍경은 이국의 관광속에 특별한 휴식과 기쁨을 더해준다.

한반도의 두배 조금 넘은 인구 4,050만명으로 또 외국 관광객이 연간 5,000만명이 넘친다는 마드리드의 호화로운 왕궁과 메스키타내부 고딕성당을 관람하고. 스페인 광장안 세르반테스의 동상이 탑 중앙에 엄숙하게 자리잡고 있다. 그 뒤엔 애마(愛馬) 로시난데를 타고있는 돈키호테와 산초판사의 웅장한 동상이 멋지게 서 있다.

프라도미술관으로 갔다. 난 미술에 대해선 문외한이지만 많은 작품중

특히 '고야(Goya)의 고뇌의 그림'은 광적이고 비틀거리는 비합리적인 모습, 내면의 모습을 느껴보기도 했다. 관객 3,000여명을 수용한다는 웅장한 라스 벤따스 투우장으로 갔다. 555~600kg의 검은 황소가 투우장 안으로 겁없이 거만한 모습으로 걸어나온다. 투우사들과의 아찔아찔한 쇼가 벌어지는 순간순간속의 잔인성을 보면서 투우사의 창칼에 애처롭게 쓰러지자 관객들은 흥분에 들떠 지르는 환호성이 하늘을 찌른다. 인간의 잔인함속에 왜 소로 태어나 저리 죽나, 가슴을 쓸어내리기도 했고 미국에서라면 동물 학대죄로 비난이 쏟아질텐데 스페인의 야만적이고 잔인한 투우는 영영 사라져야함을 권하고 싶어진다.

마드리드를 떠나 천연의 고도 중세 도시 톨레도로 이동 했다. 1561년 마드리드로 수도가 옮겨질때까지 톨레도는 정치, 경제, 문화, 종교 모든 면에서 스페인의 중심지였고 3면이 타호강에 둘러 쌓여있으며 중세의 모습과 이슬람교 문화의 발자취를 그대로 간직하고 있는 도시다. 또한 거리는 양팔을 벌리면 두 건물이 손끝에 닿을 만한 좁은 거리로 하늘과 땅이 닿아있는 듯한 도시속에 여러 민족과 문화가 맞대고 있는 미로의 도시 같다.

세르반 테스의 「돈키호테」를 탄생시킨 곳이며 헤밍웨이의 「누구를 위하여 종을 울리나」가 이곳 타호강을 배경으로 촬영 됐단다. 알칸다리를 건너 하나의 성같은 도시의 중심부 그 정상에 우뚝 서 있는 톨레도대성당으로 오르는 길은 어찌나 가파르고 위험천만한지 노련한 운전사가 얌전하게 운전해 간다. 차창밖으로 펼쳐진 신,구시가지의 경관은 한폭의 그림이다. 어머나! 어쩜! 감탄사가 여기저기서 자연스럽게 합창으로 이어지고 버스기사는 마음 좋게 차를 세워줘 일행이 우루루 내려 한차례씩 배경을 넣어 디카에 추억을 담느라 분주하게 움직였다.

톨레도성당은 1226년 공사를 시작하여 266년만에 완성된 건물로 길이 113m 폭 57m 중앙의 높이가 45m. 들어가는 문이 3개가 있는데 그 중 중앙의 문이 면죄의 문이고. 화려한 조각작품들이 산적해 있으며 기도실안 보물실엔 금으로 만든 성경책, 성도를 주제로한 스테인드 글러서 대 제단, 성가대실, 미술품이 진열된 복합 문화 공간임을 느낄 수 있었다. 엘 그레꼬의 걸작품의 상징인 오르가즈 백작의 장례식이 거행되었던 산토토메교회를 둘러보고 전망 좋은 식당에 앉아 스페인의 전통음식 Paella(해물이 듬뿍들은 볶은밥과 비슷함)와 붉은 와인을 곁들여 점심을 먹고 마드리드로 되돌아가 하루밤을 더 묵었다. 다음날 조식후 마드리드 공항으로 이동, 이륙 1시간 20분만에 바르셀로나에 도착했다,

이상기온으로 날씨가 추워 겹겹이 옷을 껴입고 시내관광을 시작으로 세계적인 건축 예술가 가우디의 걸작품인 구엘공원으로 갔다. 구엘공원은 정말 특이한 아름다운 조각과 색상도 화려한 둥근원이 디자인 위주로 구성되어 있으며 역시 가우디의 작품인 성가족성당은 한창 증축과 보수공사중(2025년에야 완공된단다) 관광객에 밀려 발걸음을 옮기기가 어찌나 힘들었는지. 도시 전체가 가우디의 박물관이라고 할만큼 너무나 아름다웠다.

에스파냐광장을 지나 1992년 바르셀로나 올림픽에서 영광의 금메달을 목에건 황영조선수가 뛰었던 몬쥬익언덕을 따라오르며 자랑스런 황영조 동상앞에 선명한 태극기가 조각되어 있어 마음 뿌듯했다. 까딸루냐 미술관은 성당의 벽화와 제단화가 수집되어 전시되어 있다고 하는데 이미 관람시간이 끝나 아쉬움만 남기고. 스페인의 명동거리라 할수 있는 LasRamblar거리에선 집시들의 표적이 된다고 가이드가 겁을 주어 잔뜩 긴장하기도 했다.

이곳의 사람들은 모두 인생을 즐기기에 바쁜것 처럼 수많은 행위 예술가들이 모여있고 선물가게, 먹걸이 속에서도 특히 가게에 길게길게 걸려있는 돼지허벅지 하몬(스페인의 Original ham)이 눈길을 끈다. 꽃가게가 즐비하고 어깨를 툭툭치고도 아무렇치않게 걸어가는 사람들의 홍수로 낭

만이 물씬 풍기는 거리다.

관광이 몰려오는 나라, 멋진 인상과 추억을 불러주는 나라. 카페 거리에서 흘러나오는 슬픔과 향수, 그리움등의 주된 감성이 뒤섞여 여행자의 온몸을 휘어잡는 색다른 음색의 파두(Fado=포르투갈의 전통가요)선율과 드높은 초원의 올리브나무들, 예쁜꽃으로 장식된 발코니가 아름다운 낯선 마을의 골목골목들 그곳서 만난사람들의 미소를 떠올려보며 지중해 연안에 있는 나라 포르투갈, 스페인에서 8박 9일간의 여행동안 집시들의 공격없이 무사히 마칠 수 있도록 보호하여 주신 하나님의 무한한 사랑에 감사한다.

일상이 단조로울때면 추억속의 여행을 떠올리며 마냥 미소짓게 되겠지.

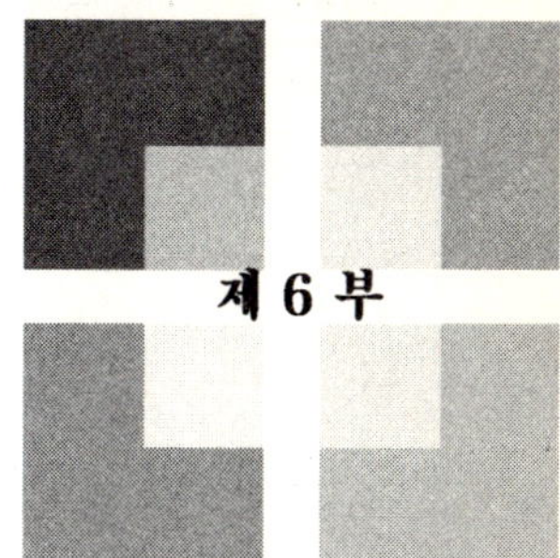

제 6 부

수필집 평설

문학의 요건 두루 갖춘 수필 돋보여

박 진 환
(문학평론가 · 문학박사)

1. 前提

수필이 '붓가는 대로', '붓을 따라서' 쓴 글이란 것은 누구나 알고 있는 수필의 ABC에 속한다. 그리고 특수한 개인적인 주제를 자유로운 수법에 의해서 산문으로 표현하는 적당한 길이의 글이란 것도 역시 정의의 ABC에 속한다.

그러나 수필이 개성적, 심경적, 경험적 글인 개성의 문학이라는 점과, 비록 산문으로 쓰여지기는 하나 산문정신에 투철한 산문문학이라는 점과, 수필이 무형식의 문학이기는 하나 기교적 미를 추구하고, 유머나 위트, 그리고 비평정신과 같은 요소들을 생명으로 하는, 심미적 가치와 철학적 가치를 조화롭게 표출해야 한다는 것은 ABC에 속하지 않는다.

수필이 비록 붓가는 대로, 아무런 형식에 구애받지 않고 써내려간 글이라 해도 문학의 장르라는 점을 간과해서는 안된다는 뜻이다. 부룩스가 지적한 바대로 독자에게 쾌락을 줄 수 있는 방법으로 인간의 사상과 감정을 지적으로 배열한 기록이 문학이라는 점을 간과해서는 안된다는 뜻인데 궁극적으로 문학은 인간의 정서적 표현의 예술이기 때문이다.

수필이 대표적인 문학장르의 하나라는 것은 바로 문학을 성립시키는 조건으로서의 쾌락의 제공과, 쾌락을 제공하기 위해서는 사상과 감정을 조화롭게 형상으로 재구성 했을 때만 가능하다는 점에서 붓가는대로와 무형식의 형식만으로는 수필문학의 여러 여건을 다 충족했다고는 할 수 없게 된다.

흔히 수필을 보고, 느끼고, 생각한 것을 그때그때 붓가는 대로 써 놓으면 수필이 되는 것으로 착각하기 쉽다. 그러나 수필이 문학으로서의 역할을 수행하기 위해서는 앞서 지적한 개성 · 산문 · 무형식과 함께 유머 · 위트 · 비평정신이 곁들여져 있어야 하고, 동시에 심미적 · 철학적 가치가 추구되거나 내재해 있어야 한다.

이러한 전제는 유설자님의 수필을 조명하기 위해 동원한 이론에 기초한 것들로서 유설자님이 이러한 전제 조건들을 얼마만큼 자신의 수필에 실천하고 있고, 또 실천함으로써 얼마만큼 문학적 성과를 거두고 있느냐를 구명하는데 기여할 것으로 본다.

2. 유설자님의 수필이 지니는 특성

수필집 『도레미파솔라시도의 합창』은 몇가지 특성을 지니고 있다고 보여진다.

그 하나는 혈통 · 인륜의식을 통한 가족애이고 두 번째로는 자연친화력을 통한 인생배우기, 셋째로는 긍정적 삶을 통한 행복의 추구, 네 번째로는 이민생활의 극복과 함께 살아온 축복의 발견, 그리고 끝으로는 세계 각지를 돌아본 여행수필로 그 특성들은 집약될 것으로 본다.

이를 중심으로 작품을 제시, 지니고 있는 특성들을 구체화 했을 때 유설자님의 수필의 본질이랄까, 수필로서의 문학적 가치랄까 향기랄까는 그 모습을 극명히 드러낼 것으로 본다.

유설자님의 수필은 다양한 소재들에 의해 다양한 내용으로 전개되고 있다. 그러나 그 중에서도 중심자리에 놓을 수 있는 것이 혈통의식을 통한 가족애라고 보여진다. 그것은 『도레미파솔라시도의 합창』 이라는 수필집 제목에서도 잘 암시되고 있다. 도레미파솔라시도는 각기 높낮이를 달리한 음계의 소리값이 아니라 여덟 손주들을 여덟 음계를 빌어 나타낸 것으로서 수필 「도레미파솔라시도의 합창」 일부를 제시하면 이점 보다 극명해 질 것으로 본다. "도레미파솔라시도의 네 손자, 네 손녀. 여덟 명의 손주들이 머리가 크고 키가 자라 건강함속에서 서로서로에게 감사하며 우애있게 서로 도우며 성장하기를 바라는 마음이다. 내 주위의 많은 분들이 딸 둘에서 손주가 여덟 명이라고 하면 모두 어머나! 왜? 그렇게 많이 낳아요? 하고 놀란다. 그러면 나의 대답은 합창단을 만든데요 다."에서 볼 수 있듯이 유설자님의 진한 혈통 및 가족애를 읽게 해주고 있다. 작품을 제시했을 때 이해를 도울 것으로 본다.

가) 이제 우리 6남매는 미국에 넷, 한국에 둘 비록 이산가족이지만 모두 잘살고 있는데 정작 효도받으셔야할 어머니는 우리 곁에 더 이상 안 계신다. 이제는 아버지도 이 세상에 안계신다. 서둘러 달려갔을 때 아버지는 혼수 상태에 계셨다. 잠시 정상으로 돌아오셔서 주위에 앉은 아들, 며느리, 딸, 사위들을 둘러보시고 눈을 감으셨다.

나) 가족 캠프장 안에 있는 5베드룸 콘도에 온 가족이 도착해 짐들을 풀며 바삐 움직인다. 난 손자 손녀들과 백사장에 나가 앉아 장난감 삽으로 모래를 퍼 담으며 모래 위에 그림도 그리며 모래성도 쌓고 모래를 깊게 파 고인 물에 조그마한 발들을 담그며 좋아라 깔깔댄다. 물위에 떠서 올려다보는 파아란 하늘에 떠다니는 뭉게 구름이 어찌나 아름답고 평화로운지 마치 선녀가 되어 구름 위를 나는 기분이다.

예시한 수필 가)는 「어머니를 그리는 마음」의 일부이고, 나)는 「바닷가에서의 행복」 일부로서 가)가 혈통의식을 발상으로 했다면 나)는 가족애를 발상으로 쓰여졌다고 본다. 아버지의 임종을 기다리며 둘러 앉은 6남매를 통해서 읽을 수 있는 혈통의식이나, 주위에 둘러앉은 아들, 며느리, 딸, 사위들을 통해 이를 보다 구체화한 혈통의 연계맥락을 통해 진한 혈통의식을 읽게 해주는 것이 예시한 수필 가)다.

그런가 하면 여름방학을 맞아 찾아온 손자 · 손녀와 온가족이 함께 캠프를 치고 바닷가에서 하룻밤을 지낸 행복한 가족 나들이를 보여주는 것이 예시한 수필 나)다.

예시 수필 외에도 「봄의 향기와 그리움의 파도」, 「벚꽃 속의 봄 방학」, 「젊은 날의 추억」, 「추억을 불러준 테입」을 비롯한 여러 편의 수필도 같은 맥락에 있대어 있어 역시 혈통 · 가족애를 발상으로 쓰여졌음을 보여주고 있다.

문제는 이러한 수필들이 단순한 소제가 아닌 인류의식으로 확대되면서 심미적 설득력을 지니고 있다는데 있다. 전제에서 밝혔듯이 문학은 감동을 체험하게 했을 때 언어예술로 인정받게 되는데 그것이 심미적 설득력으로서 수필도 예외는 아니다. 이점에서 유설자님의 수필이 심미적 설득력으로 작용하고 있다는 것은 혈통 · 가족의식이라는 단순한 소제주의적 한계를 극복한 것이 되어주게 된다. 그리고 그 이유는 그것이 혈통의식이

건, 가족애이건 의식의 다양한 여과과정을 거쳐 사랑의 진솔성으로 재구성되고, 재구성의 결구력이 끈끈한 사랑으로 접착되는 인류애로 확대되는 공감대를 획득해 내고 있기 때문이다.

두 번째로 지적될 수 있는 특성이랄까, 중심자리에 놓을 수 있는 것이 자연친화력이라고 할까, 자연을 통한 인생 및 자아 읽기라고나 할까를 보여주는 순수자연감정이다.

가) 가을은 화려한 결실의 계절! 그러나 이 결실은 세월이 흐른다고 그냥 영그는 것이 아니다. 씨앗 하나가 열매를 맺기까지 봄, 여름, 그리고 가을에 이르는 자연의 변화도 이겨야하고 씨앗이 땅에 뿌리를 내리고 자라는 자아변신의 아픔도 견디어야 하는 것이다. 우리가 살아가는 것도 자연의 이치와 다를 바 없다.

특히나 우리 이민의 삶을 살아가노라면 어려운 고개가 높고 낮음이 험하고, 힘들때가 얼마나 많은가. 순간순간에 닥치는 어려움을 잘 견디며 좌절하지 말고 열심히 살아간다는 것은 행복을 말하는 것이고 기쁨을 말하는 것이 아니겠는가.

나) 또한 가을은 누군가의 마음에 내 마음을 새겨 넣고 싶은 계절. 누군가에게 편지를 쓰고 싶은 계절이다. 사랑하는 사람에게는 내 사랑의 마음을. 미워하는 사람에게는 화해의 마음을. 나보다 가난한 사람에게는 따뜻한 축복의 마음을 전하고 싶어진다. 시간에 쫓기어 만나지 못하는 친척이나 친구가 어느날 나의 편지를 받는다면 그들은 얼마나 즐거워할 것인가. 그립고 보고 싶은 친척, 친구의 얼굴을 떠올리며 말하듯 글을 쓰는 낭만. 이 가을에 흠뻑 젖어보자.

예시된 수필 가)는 「가을의 노래」의 일부이고 나)는 「가을 단상」의 일부이다. 같은 소재를 다루고 있으면서도 전자는 결실의 계절을 중심으로 자연의 섭리나 철리같은 것을 읽게 해주고 후자는 가을이 환기시키는 정서적 심경을 사랑과 미움과 용서와 화해와 같은 순수 자연 감정으로 여과시켜 형상으로 빚어내주고 있다.

친 자연 감정이라고나 할까, 자연 친화력이라고나 할까, 그도 아니면 자연동화나 자연 경도와 같은 이러한 자연성은 매우 값진 것들이라 할 수 있다. 그것은 도시문명이나 물질주의에 잘 길들여진 현대인들이 어쩌면 자연을 잃었거나, 외면하거나, 아니면 자연의 질서밖으로 내동댕이 쳐 진 체 살아가고 있기 때문이다. 이 점에서 보면 자연친화력의 수필들은 유설자님의 자연감정이 오염되지 않은 순수로 여과됐음을 보여주는 것이 된다.

세 번째로 간과할 수 없는 특성의 하나는 건강한 삶과 삶을 통한 긍정적 생명의식을 중심으로 한 일련의 수필들이다. 건강한 삶이 가져다 주는 감사할 줄 아는 생활 태도, 일상적 삶을 통해 삶의 진실을 깨우치며 즐거워하는 태도, 이웃과 더불어 사는 즐거움에의 체험, 그리고 힘겨웠던 이민의 삶이 가져다 주는 생의 애환을 담고 있는 수필들도 유설자님의 수필중 중요한 자리를 차지하고 있다.

가) 하나님의 주신 고귀한 삶을 살면서 오늘로 결혼 36주년 기념일이기도 한 우리 부부는 힘들고 어렵기도 했고 보람도 있었던 이민생활 33년을 회상하며 늘 건강 지켜주셔서 오늘을 살게 하시고 살아있음으로 가능성의 의미를 가질 수 있도록 하시는 하나님의 크신 축복에 감사의 눈물이 고이기도 했다.

나) 향기 가득한 커피를 타서 마시니 그 따뜻함이 손길을 타고 오르며 마음은 어느사이 발랄한 생동감으로 꿈틀거린다. 고장났던 히터는 기술자의 도움으로 방안 가득 더운 공기를 뿜어대기 시작한다. 우리의 삶에도 한겨울에 히터가 고장 난 것 같은 하나의 가치에 열심히 매달려 있다가 잘 풀리지 않을 때 우울함 속에서 한참을 허우적대며 방황하는 마음의 온기가 꺼지는 날이 있을지 모른다. 그래도 우리는 무던히 마음을 다

스러 다시 불을 피워 올려야 하는 노력의 날들이기를 바란다.

다) 장기간 집을 비우게 된다고 하니까 집안에 있는 화초에 물주기, 잔디깎기, 낙엽 긁기 등 아무 염려 말고 즐겁게 다녀오란다. 서로 믿고 도울 수 있는 이웃이 있어 살아가는 것이 즐겁고, 그들의 싱글벙글 행복한 미소가 있어 이웃인 우리도 행복함에 젖으니 감사하다.

예시된 수필 가)는 「감사하는 삶」의 일부이고, 나)는 「한 겨울 고장 난 히터」의 일부, 다)는 「이웃사촌」의 각각 일부이다.

예시 수필 가)는 매우 건강한 삶을 보여주고 있다. 힘들고 어려웠던 이민의 삶이었지만, 이를 긍정적으로 받아들이면서 하나님이 주신 고귀한 삶으로 감사할 줄 아는 삶의 건전하고 건강함을 보여주고 있다.

나)는 일상적 삶을 통해 항용 경험할 수 있는 생활주변의 단면을 제단해 다 따뜻한 인인애를 바탕으로 재구성 해주고 있다.

그리고 다)는 장기간 집을 비우면서 이웃에게 맡기고 가는, 또 이를 마다않고 맡아주는 이웃간의 믿음과 사랑을 진솔하게 보여주고 있는데 긍정적 삶과 인인애, 그리고 믿음을 가지고 살아가는 삶에서 따뜻한 온기가 느껴진다.

이 외에도 수필 「꽃다운 시절의 추억을 불러준 영화들」이 보여주는 긍정적 삶, 「생명의 고마움과 축복」에서 읽을 수 있는 생명에의 외경과 감사, 「배움의 기쁨」에서의 이웃과 더불어 살아가는 공존의 삶등도 건강한 작가의 삶을 여실히 보여주고 있다.

끝으로 또 하나의 비중으로 다가오는 것이 여행수필이다. 수필 「뜨루히요의 풍경」, 「아테네 그리고 신비의 카파도키아에서」를 비롯한 10여편의 수필들은 일종의 기행수필이다.

기행수필은 흔히 현지 답사나 르뽀가 되거나 주마간산격인 단면들만 제시하기 마련인데 반해 유설자님의 기행수필은 폭넓고 깊이있게 다룬 일종의 기행문 성격을 지니고 있다. 외양이나 눈에 스치는 것만을 스케치하거나 스넵으로 담아온 그런 기행 수필이 아니라, 현장의 리얼리티는 물론, 역사성, 전통성, 특수성 등을 고루 담아 마치 현장을 파노라마로 펼쳐주는 것 같아 흥미를 배가 시켜주고 있다.

이상은 수필집 『도레미파솔라시도의 합창』을 주마간산격으로 훑어본 일종의 독후감 성격을 지닌 해설로서 몇 개의 중심을 관류하고 있는 특성들을 찾아 언급한 것이다. 그 결과 대부분의 수필들이 수필이 문학이 되는 요건들을 고루 갖추고 있어 신뢰가 갔고, 또 설득력을 지니고 있어 감동을 수반하게 했는데 이점이 유설자님의 수필집 『도레미파솔라시도의 합창』이 거둔 수필의 성과로 제시될 수 있다고 본다.

수필집 출간에 박수를 보낸다.

수필가 유설자 님은 1942년 평안북도 신의주에서 출생. 1961년 수도여자고등학교 졸업했고, 1972년 도미했다. 2005년 『조선문학』에 수필이 당선돼 등단했고, 2006년 해외문학(LA)에 수필당선. 워싱턴 여류 수필가 협회 부회장으로 있으며, 조선문학 문인회 회원, 해외문인협회 회원, 미주 문예동우회 회원으로 활동하고 있다. 현재 미주 한국일보(Washington, D.C.)에 기고 수필가로 집필에 전념하고 있다.

· *E-mail : suljayoo@hanmail.net*

도레미파솔라시도의 합창

2008년 11월 20일 인쇄
2008년 11월 30일 발행

지은이 / 유설자
발행인 / 박진환
펴낸곳 / 조선문학사
등록번호 / 1-2733
주소 · 110-092 서울 서대문구 홍제2동 96-4
대표전화 / 730-2255
팩스 / 723-9373

ISBN 89-91811-90-6 03810

정가 15,000원